In the Beginning

In the Beginning

Creation and the Priestly History

Robert B. Coote
and
David Robert Ord

FORTRESS PRESS   MINNEAPOLIS

IN THE BEGINNING
Creation and the Priestly History

Cover and internal design by Jim Gerhard
Cover illustration: detail of *The Creation of Light* by Paul Gustave Doré

Library of Congress Cataloging-in-Publication Data

Coote, Robert B., 1944–
  In the beginning : creation and the priestly history / Robert B. Coote and David Robert Ord.
    p.   cm.
  Includes bibliographical references.
  ISBN 0-8006-2527-7 (alk. paper)
    1. Creation—Biblical teaching.   2. Bible. O.T. Genesis I—Criticism, interpretation, etc.   3. P document (Biblical criticism)
  I. Ord, David Robert.   II. Title.
  BS1199.C73C66   1991
  222'.1106—dc20   91-36859
                                                        CIP

The paper used in this publication meets the minimum requirements of American National Standard for Information Sciences—Permanence of Paper for Printed Library Materials, ANSI Z329.48–1984.   ∞ ™

Manufactured in the U.S.A.   AF 1-2527

95   94   93   92   91   1   2   3   4   5   6   7   8   9   10

On the first day God created potatoes.
On the second day God created potatoes.
On the third day also God created potatoes.
And on the fourth and fifth day God created potatoes.
So on the sixth day why did he have to create us?—I ask you.

Yefim Magazanik,
Ukrainian Jewish village tinker, in *Kommissar*,
screenplay by Alexander Askoldov, 1987 (1967).

Contents

Preface   ix

Introduction   1

1 What Creation Stories Are Really About   5

2 More Than One Creation Story   19

3 Who Wrote Genesis One?   29

4 Revising the Official History   39

5 Everything Falls into Place   49

6 Living in the Lap of Luxury   57

7 Women: Keep Out   67

8 How We Got Our Work Week   77

9 A World Centered in a Tent   95

10 The Opulent and the Messy   105

11 The Creation of Order   117

12 The Priestly Account in the New Testament   135

Epilogue: Creation in Our Time   159

For Further Reading   165

Author Index   179

Subject Index   181

Preface

This book is the third by the authors to deal with the major strands of the first four books of the Bible. The first was on J (Coote and Ord, *The Bible's First History,* Fortress, 1989), the second on E (Coote, *In Defense of Revolution,* Fortress, 1991), and now this one attempts to explain the basic features of the priestly stratum in the Tetrateuch, known to biblical scholars as P.

This book differs from its companions in the series in two significant respects. First, rather than developing a new view of P, it presents mostly rather well established propositions. However, since these pertain to various disparate topics in scriptural studies, they have not appeared together and in relationship to one another in one place. We believe that to understand any of the discrete topics related to the priestly strand of the Tetrateuch, such as creation, Sabbath, or sacrifice, it is necessary to have a basic grasp of all of the strand's significant aspects.

Second, we intend this book as a contribution to the discussion regarding a concern that does not spring directly from a historical study of the priestly strand, but is a part of the American culture within which we write. This is the popular notion that the world was created in seven days as the Bible says. For those who wish to inform themselves regarding this issue, there is much scientific literature refuting creationism, showing that the world was not created the way Genesis 1 says it was (see the suggested readings under the heading of Introduction). What is needed in addition is a book on Genesis 1 itself: if it is not a description of the creation of the world, then what is it? This book attempts to provide a full and critical answer to that question, so that whatever we are discussing in the priestly history at a particular point will be related back to Genesis 1, as indeed the priestly writers probably wished anyway.

Our debt to other scholars will be evident from the notes and bibliography. A particularly important critical reading of the manuscript in preparation was provided by Marvin L. Chaney. Students and parishioners likewise communicated their criticisms, for which we always tried to express our gratitude. Polly Coote graciously prepared the indices.

Introduction

Is the first chapter of Genesis an accurate description of the way the world came into being? This question has confused, bewildered, and divided millions of people who want to believe in the Bible but who have been told that its account of creation is in conflict with the findings of modern science.

For many, the validity of the Bible is at stake in the question of whether creation happened the way the opening chapter of Genesis describes. Genesis 1 says God created the world in six days, and for them this is authoritative. They argue that either the Bible is historically and scientifically accurate in every detail, or it cannot be relied upon at all. For the person who takes such a position on the issue of biblical authority, there is only one response: to agree or disagree. Either you believe or you do not.

There is another question we might put to the text. Instead of asking whether we believe the account of creation in the first chapter of Genesis is accurate, we might ask what it *means*.

The question of meaning places the discussion about Genesis 1 within a quite different framework from that of whether it is authoritative in a historical and scientific sense. It is a question that calls for a more complex answer than a simple yes or no. The Bible was written long before our time, in a place quite different from our own, in a culture alien to the one most of us are familiar with, and in a language foreign to speakers of English. How can we be sure that Genesis 1 meant the same thing to the person who first wrote it as it does to many of us?

In the modern world, the creation issue is one of how and when our world and universe came into being. We humans have a sense of time—an awareness that this minute is different from the last, today different from yesterday, this year different from last year, and that the future will differ from the present in a similar way. Our sense of time leads us to ask: If we keep going back and back in time, what do we come to? Where is the beginning, and what happened back then? Without much effort, anyone, even the most learned scientist, will find themselves wondering about a time they can know nothing about. In fact, scientists ask any number of questions about origins that they simply have no way at present of answering. This is especially true of the question "Why?" which is beyond the scope of telescopes and test tubes. Scientists leave these questions aside in favor of questions about realities that they *are* in a position to investigate.

In writing about creation, was the author of Genesis 1 concerned with the same things as the scientist in the modern era? Was the *how* and *when* of creation his principal interest, or was he concerned with issues that stem from the question of *why* the created order is as it is—issues that we today might never think of discussing in the context of creation?

In modern science, to talk about the beginning we have to assume that the world of the beginning, of which we have no direct experience, was in significant ways the same as, or comparable to, the world of the present, of which we do have direct experience. People have little difficulty making this assumption. It is after all reasonable to assume a certain continuity in time, which itself is part of our experience. The description of the beginning, then, tends to be limited to those aspects of our experience of the present, mysterious though they may be, that someone can actually understand.

Historians face the same limitation. Their view of the past is inevitably influenced by their view of the present, which affects how they weigh the evidence and even what they regard as significant in history in the first place.

Most today are aware that people in different countries and cultures have widely divergent views on any number of issues. We who live in the United States see things quite differently from the peoples of Latin America, China, the Middle East, or Africa. If within the same generation we must go to great lengths to understand the other's point of view, it is clearly no easy task to discover how peoples removed from us by thousands of years thought and felt about issues. In many cases we may never know how those of a bygone era thought. Indeed, the less known about earlier times, the more talk about those times will be talk about the present. This is especially true of the unknown beginning, which we must talk of entirely in terms of the known present. This assumption of continuity is also inherent in our interest in the beginning, for the most common reason for thinking about the beginning is to understand the present better.

Even as the scientist and historian were not present at the beginning and must speak of creation in terms of the known world, so too the writer of Genesis 1 was not present at the moment of creation. Like us, he knew nothing directly about the historical origins of the material and biological world around him. On what, then, did he base his creation story?

We could answer this question in terms of biblical authority, and the usual answer would be that God told the author of Genesis 1 how creation occurred. The issue is then a simple matter of belief or disbelief. But if the question is answered in terms of what the creation story *means,* the issue is different. In the context of meaning, the author's concern would be with the world in which he lived, and with the political, social, and cultural issues of his time. The creation story is a way of talking about matters that were of concern to those living in the era when it was composed. In this view, Genesis 1 and science do have one thing in common: they both talk about the past in terms of the present.

To understand the view of creation in either science or Genesis 1, we may ask in each case what characteristics of the present are utilized to describe the past. In both cases the present has its own cultural and moral qualities, in which power, rights, worldview, and authority all play a role. The truth of either the scientific view of creation or the view of Genesis 1 depends on the validity of how it interprets its present, and hence on the validity of the values by which we assess that present.

In the debate over the truth of Genesis 1, little attention has been given to the values and politics inherent in this and other biblical accounts of creation. Learning something of the values and political assumptions of Genesis 1 makes it possible for us to perceive its truth on its own terms, rather than superimposing on it the issues of cosmology, paleontology, geology, biology, and so forth, involved in the modern debate.

Biblical versions of creation make next to nothing of creation in the scientific sense. Their main concern is to describe order, structure, sequence, and relation, not the creation of matter per se. They differ among themselves and from other creation stories beyond the covers of the Bible not in terms of the origin of the substance of things, but in terms of the structure or order of things. Creation in this sense is about world structures and orders, in which not only religion but also politics, economics, and social relations play a part. We will tend to ask, therefore, not simply how did creation occur in one account in contrast to another, but what particular order of the world of the writer is implied by a given account of creation.

Many versions of creation written and used by other people in other places during Bible times are known to historians. To learn the meaning of Genesis 1, we will begin not with Genesis 1 itself, but with those ancient texts that have close similarities to Genesis 1. After looking at these in their contexts, and then at the probable historical contexts of a number of biblical accounts of creation, we shall investigate the particular setting, both textual and historical, of the most famous of all ancient accounts of how things all began. Since many readers are not familiar with either the extrabiblical or biblical texts to which we refer, and since they form such an important foundation for what will follow, we found it necessary to quote from them extensively, a practice that some may find tedious. We ask such readers to bear with us in the first two chapters.

Much of what is said here is already well known and available in reference works and textbooks. But the basics have not previously been put together as they are here, and even those who are aware of them often do not relate them enough to the account of creation in Genesis 1. It is perhaps difficult to believe that a subject as familiar as the biblical story of creation has to do with subjects as unfamiliar as those to be discussed here.

1

What Creation Stories Are Really About

In the ancient Near Eastern tradition—or in any other tradition for that matter—there is no such thing as creation in general, in the sense of a scientific understanding of how matter and the universe as a whole came into being. Some particular thing, circumstance, or set of circumstances is created, not things in general.

Creation stories accounted for the things and circumstances that played a role in people's daily lives and could be about anything down to the cause of toothache. Thus one Akkadian text, an incantation against toothache, concerns a certain "worm" thought to cause severe dental pain. After the god Anu had created heaven, heaven had created earth, earth rivers, rivers canals, and canals the worm, this worm went to the gods Ea and Shamash asking for something more than figs and apricots to gnaw on. They gave him leave to "suck the blood of the tooth" and "gnaw at the base of the gums."[1] Those creation stories that addressed the really big things, the comprehensive view, dealt with people's concept of the world and encompassed their relationship to the earth, the status of people, the role of work, the function of kingship (power), and the service of gods.

The centers for writing in the ancient world were the great urban centers with their palaces and temples. Together the palace and temple represented the state, which organized the power of the dominant families in the class of wealthy landowners. The scribal class and the priestly class who conducted the services of the temples were usually

1. James B. Pritchard, *Ancient Near Eastern Texts Relating to the Old Testament,* 2d ed. (Princeton: Princeton University Press, 1955), 100–101. This work will be abbreviated *ANET.*

closely related to each other. Thus the texts that talk about creation come from these palace and temple contexts. The temple was conceived of as the palace of the god, or an earthly replica of the god's palace in the sky or underworld. The word "house" is often used for palace or temple.

The whole idea of creating a "world" depends on the scope of the world as a person conceives of it. Since creation in the ancient Near East is viewed from a particular cult[2] setting, by far the most common concept of creation is the creation of the world with the urban temple at its center and as its most important element. The temple is the focal point of creation in nearly every account available to us. Had the peasantry possessed a concept of the creation of the world, it too would have reflected their "world." The farmer's or villager's world was more modest than that of the temple-centered state, and more focused on the immediate circumstances of family safety and food production in village and countryside.

MESOPOTAMIA

The use made of creation texts, when it is known to us, reflects the world of temple. An example is a short narrative that forms the introduction to an incantation recited as part of the purification of the temple of the Babylonian god Nabu. Nabu was the god of the city of Borsippa, near Babylon. When the cult of Nabu increased in importance in the Neo-Babylonian period, Nabu was said to be a son of Marduk, the god of Babylon itself. The main theme of the creation narrative with which the incantation opens is the justification of Marduk's primacy among the Babylonian gods. This text begins as follows:

> A holy house, a house of the gods in a holy place, had not been made. A reed had not come forth, a tree had not been created. A brick had not been laid, a brick mold had not been built. A house had not been made, a city had not been built. A city had not been made, a living creature had not been placed (in it). The city of Nippur and its temple had not been built. The city of Uruk and its temple had not been built. The lagoons of the lower Euphrates and their city Eridu had not been built. A holy house, a house of

2. In popular use, the word cult today has a negative connotation, usually with reference to a religious organization that deviates from mainstream Christianity. We use it in its technical sense, meaning a religious system.

the gods, its dwelling, had not been made. All the lands were sea. The spring in the seas overflowed. Then Eridu was made, Esagila was built [Esagila was the name of the temple of Ea or Enki in Eridu. Later Marduk took on many of the features of Ea, and the temple of Marduk in Babylon was also called Esagila, as below], Esagila whose foundations Lugaldukuga laid within the lagoons. Babylon was made, Esagila was completed. The Anunnaki gods Lugaldukuga created equal. The holy city, the dwelling of their hearts' delight, they called it solemnly. Marduk constructed a reed frame on the face of the waters. He created dirt and poured it out by the reed frame. In order to settle the gods in the dwelling of their hearts' delight, he created humanity. Aruru created the seed of humanity together with Marduk. He created cattle and the living things of the steppe. He created the Tigris and Euphrates and set them in place. Their names he appropriately proclaimed. He created the grass, the rush of the marsh, the reed, and the woods. He created the grain of the field, the lands, the marshes, the canebreaks; the cow and her young, the calf; the ewe and her lamb, the sheep of the fold; the orchards and the forests; the wild sheep, the wool sheep (?). . . . Lord Marduk piled up a dam at the edge of the sea; [. . .] a swamp he made into dry land . . . he caused to be. He created the reed, he created the tree. . . in the place he created. Bricks he laid, the brick mold he built. The house he built, the city he built. The city he made, living creatures he placed therein. Nippur and its temple he built. Uruk and its temple he built.[3]

Here, as in nearly every other case known, the creation of the world is in fact the creation of a cult, the rites of a priesthood—and in every known instance, a state priesthood.

A number of elements in this narrative are common in ancient Near Eastern cult creation narratives. The condition of the world before the god creates the items of particular interest is described. The items mentioned—reed, tree, brick, and brick mold—are items of importance for the construction of the mud-brick temple. The created order arises out of the sea, whose bounds are then set so that the created order cannot later be violated. The mightiest god leads the work crew, at least nominally, to establish ownership as the prime worker on the project, even though in fact gangs of hired and forced workers did the work of building the temple. The god created humanity to do

3. Alexander Heidel, *The Babylonian Genesis* (Chicago: University of Chicago Press, 1951), 61–63. The translation has been slightly modified.

work and service in the world, particularly its cult, in place of the gods, who, like the ruling class, avoid dirt work in their palaces and temples and devote themselves to their main activities—military expeditions for the royal class, and butchery and clerical work for the priestly class. The animals created are the main fare of the cult. All this is a prelude or accompaniment to the purification or reestablishment of the cult in question, in this case in Borsippa.

A ritual text from Babylon, prescribed for the restoration of a temple, calls for offerings and hymns, and then the recitation of the following:

> When the god Anu had created the heavens, and Ea had built the Apsu, his dwelling, Ea nipped off clay in the Apsu. He created Kulla, god of bricks, for the restoration of the temples. He created the reed marsh and the forest for the work of their construction. He created the gods of carpenters and smiths, to complete the work of their construction. He created the mountains and the seas for whatever [. . . .] He created the gods of goldsmiths, smiths, engravers, and stonecutters for their works, and their rich produce for offerings [. . . .] He created the gods of grain, livestock, wine, and fruits [. . .] to provide abundant regular offerings. He created Marduk's cook and cupbearer to present their offerings. He created the king for the maintenance of the temples. He created humanity for the performance of the services of the gods.[4]

The creation of humanity is explained in more detail in the nearly complete Babylonian narrative of the creation of Esagila and its cult, named for its first two words, *Enuma elish*. In Babylonian these words mean "When above." This narrative, like most ancient creation narratives including Genesis 1, commences with a parenthetical setting of the scene, eight lines long, "When . . . ," and not until the ninth line does the main action begin, "then. . . ." The full narrative is seven tablets long. The main acts of creation do not take place until tablets five and six.

In the first tablet, the first pair of deities—the god Apsu of the fresh water and the goddess Tiamat of the salt water—produced several generations of offspring, including Anu, the sky, and Ea. In time the younger gods became unruly and bothersome to their great ancestors. Apsu determined to put a stop to their disruption of his sleep. Word

---

4. Heidel, *Babylonian Genesis*, 65–66. The translation has been slightly modified.

got to Ea of his plan. Ea, a clever god, charmed Apsu, put him to sleep, and killed him. Then "on Apsu he established his dwelling place," went in to his wife Damkina, and fathered Marduk. Marduk was a heroic child, and the gods' excitement at his birth caused further disruption and disturbed Tiamat, unreconciled at Apsu's death, day and night, until she, too, laid plans to make war against the younger gods. Tiamat created weapons and terrible monsters to wield them, and exalted Kingu at the head of her army.

As the second tablet opens, Anshar, one of the older gods, is looking for an opponent against Tiamat. He incites Ea, who, having aged since beating Apsu, is no match for Tiamat. Anu likewise goes out to battle at Anshar's behest, but he too is beaten back. Anshar is left with Marduk, who receives the advice of his father and of Anshar and readily agrees to carry out the task.

In tablet three, Marduk and Tiamat prepare for battle. The language suggests a conflict of groups or parties, not just gods:

> Tiamat held a meeting and raged furiously. All the gods went over to her, even those whom the older gods created to march at her side. They separated themselves and went over to the side of Tiamat. They were angry, they plotted, not resting day or night. They took up the fight, fuming and raging. They held a meeting and planned the conflict.[5]

These words remind one of the infighting of elite factions for the spoils of the taxing and cultic prerogatives of the state. Marduk represents not just the creator god of the state, but a particular party of Babylon who regard it as their right to withstand the threat of overthrow from opposing factions.

The great battle takes place in tablet four. Marduk wins. At the end of tablet four and in tablet five, on top of and out of Tiamat's dead body, the same salt sea we have already seen in other narratives of creation, Marduk creates the world of earth and sky. After a major break, the sixth tablet takes up the subject of who is going to do the work in Marduk's world. He thinks up a plan worthy of clever Ea and proceeds to inform the old warrior:

> Blood will I form and cause bone to be. Then will I set up humanity; "human" shall be its name. Yea, I will create humanity, "human."

5. Heidel, *Babylonian Genesis*, 26, 31.

Upon him shall the services of the gods be imposed, that they may be at rest.

Ea proposed a variation on Marduk's plan:

Let a brother of the gods be delivered up; let him be destroyed and humans fashioned. Let the great gods assemble here, let the party guilty of revolt be delivered up, but let the other rebel gods be established.

Marduk liked the idea of executing the ringleader of the revolt. He put Ea's plan into effect:

With Kingu's blood they created humanity. Ea imposed the services of the gods upon them and set the gods free.

The gods were so delighted with their freedom that when their places in the world order had been assigned, they decided to do Marduk a favor in return:

"What shall be the sign of our gratitude before thee? Come, let us make something whose name shall be called 'sanctuary.' It shall be a dwelling for our rest at night [note the allusion back to the very beginning of the narrative, where Apsu and Tiamat were having trouble sleeping due to the disruption of the younger gods]. Come, let us repose therein. There let us erect a throne platform, a seat with a back support.[6] On the day that we arrive in festival array, we will repose in it." When Marduk heard this, his countenance shone exceedingly, like the day, and he said, "So let Babylon be, whose construction ye have desired. Let its brickwork be fashioned, and call it a sanctuary." The gods wielded the digging hoe. One year they made bricks for it. When the second year arrived, they raised the top of Esagila on high, level with the cosmic waters seen above the sky. After they had built the lofty stagetower of the Apsu, they established an abode therein for Marduk, Enlil, and Ea. He sat down before them in majesty.[7]

In the conclusion of tablet six and for all of tablet seven, the gods build themselves chapels, then declare the praises of Marduk enthroned before them and recite his fifty names, or epithets, which present him as the greatest of the gods and hence his cult in Babylon as the center of the world.

6. Not a common piece of furniture in those times.
7. Heidel, *Babylonian Genesis,* 46–49.

Another Babylonian text that presents the creation of humanity in similar terms is the *Atrahasis,* named for its hero, who like Noah was the survivor of the great flood. Though not a narrative of creation in the full sense, it is likewise concerned with the way the gods were relieved when humans were created to do their work for them, and in its presentation of the creation of humans in a birthlike process it reveals its interest in the cult and its relation to "women who bear and women who do not bear." It begins, "When gods like (later) humans bore the work basket and did all the toil. . . ." The lesser gods doing work for greater gods rebelled at their condition. Ea suggested a plan. The leader of the gods' rebellion should be slaughtered, his blood mixed with clay, and out of the mixture humans created. This plan was carried out, though in a way that established the course of pregnancy and childbirth as well. When humanity had been created, they were duly put to work for the cults of Mesopotamia:

> With picks and spades they built the shrines, they built the big canal banks—for food for people, for the sustenance of the gods.[8]

When later the humans themselves multiplied and began to disrupt the gods, the god Enlil decided to send a plague against the humans. Ea advised them to withhold their cult offerings from all gods except the god of plague, and the latter held off and the humans were not forced to suffer. As the humans continued on their disruptive course, Enlil got the rain god Adad to hold back his rain to cause a famine. When the humans serviced his cult only, he surreptitiously arranged for enough rain to get through to save the humans. Enlil eventually reinstated the drought, with express orders that no god was to violate his command. Ea's human protégé Atrahasis, the king, was busy entreating his god. When Ea made fun of Enlil's command, Enlil decided he had better do something quite different and sudden. He determined to end the drought with a violent flood.

The episodes that follow have been known for over a hundred years in the version presented in the famous ancient epic of Gilgamesh. Ea was able to warn Atrahasis of the impending flood, so that the human could build a boat in order to rescue himself. As the flood waters subside, after having killed virtually all humanity, Ea mollifies Enlil

8. W. G. Lambert and A. R. Millard, *Atra-hasis: The Babylonian Story of the Flood* (Oxford: Clarendon Press, 1969), 64–67.

and some arrangement is made to continue the human race, but with fewer numbers than before. The reduced numbers derived from a cultic order that included several classes of priestesses who were forbidden to bear children:

> Establish *ugbabtu*-women, *entu*-women, and *igitsitu*-women, and let
> them be taboo and so stop childbirth.[9]

The reason for this limitation on childbirth probably has to do with the cult's control of the wealth of important families in the state. Another possibility is that the concept of celibate or infertile religious expresses the awareness of the need for population control in the ancient Mesopotamian city.[10]

The myth of Enki (Ea) and Ninmah relates the same circumstance that the gods once had to do the work for their cults. The beginning of this text is fragmentary:

> On that day, when heaven . . . from earth, on that night, when
> heaven . . . from earth, in that year, the year when the destinies
> were fixed, when the Anunna gods were born, when the divine
> mothers were taken as brides, when the divine mothers were allotted
> their places in heaven and earth, when the divine mothers . . . gave
> birth, at that time the gods were bound to labor for their sustenance,
> all the gods stood to the work, the younger gods lifted the basket
> [did corvée work]. Digging out the canals, with their earth the gods
> heaped up the Harali. The gods grumbled and complained about
> it. At the time the most-wise, the one who had formed all the great
> gods, Enki that is, lay sleeping on his bed in the hollow of the
> Apsu, a place whose interior no god has seen.[11]

The tie between the relief of the gods by the creation of working humans and the cult is made explicit in the following narrative of creation. The *uzumua* referred to was the sacred temple precinct of the city Nippur. The world has been ordered, and the Anunnaki gods are advising Enlil on "what else shall we create?"

> In Uzumua, the bond of heaven and earth, let us slay two Lamga
> (craft working) gods. With their blood let us create humanity. The
> services of the gods be their portion for all times, to maintain the

9. Lambert and Millard, 102–3.
10. Anne Draffkorn Kilmer, "The Mesopotamian Concept of Overpopulation and its Solution as Reflected in the Mythology," *Orientalia* 41 (1972): 160–77, especially pp. 171–73.
11. Translation by Richard Caplice.

> boundary ditch, to place the hoe and the basket into their hands, for the dwelling of the great gods, which is fit to be an exalted sanctuary, to mark off field from field for all times, to maintain the boundary ditch, to give the trench its right course, to maintain the boundary stone, to water the four regions of the earth, to raise plants in abundance, rains. . . .

Following a gap, the text continues:

> To maintain the boundary, to fill the granary . . . to make the field of the Anunnaki produce plentifully, to increase the abundance in the land, to celebrate the festivals of the gods, to pour out cold water in the great house of the gods, which is fit to be an exalted sanctuary.[12]

A Sumerian creation text from several centuries earlier shows many similarities, and refers likewise to the creation of the order out of which the temple of Nippur arose:

> When Enlil had made the fitting shine out, the lord, whose decisions on destiny are unchangeable, Enlil, so the seed of the land could come out, he hastened to make heaven and earth separate so that the seed should spring forth from the land, so that Uzumua could cause the first humans to spring forth. He bound up the gash in Duranki,[13] he set hoe there and day broke. He set working assignments . . . stretched out his hand to the carrying basket, and he praised the hoe and brought it into Uzumua. He put the first of the humans into (the furrow). Enlil looked with favor on the people . . . made the people grasp the hoe.[14]

EGYPT

The same relation between creation and cult that dominates the tradition of written creation narratives in the ancient world can be seen in Egyptian literature, the other great corpus of the ancient Near East. One Egyptian cult that used the idea of creation was the cult of the supposed continued life of noble persons after their death. Many

---

12. Heidel, *Babylonian Genesis*, 68–70.
13. Duranki means "the bond of heaven and earth" and designates the temple precinct of Nippur just as Uzumua does. See Tikva Frymer-Kensky, "The Planting of Man: A Study in Biblical Imagery," in *Love and Death in the Ancient Near East: Essays in Honor of Marvin H. Pope*, eds. John H. Marks and Robert M. Good, (Guilford, Conn.: Four Quarters Publishing Company, 1987), 129–36, especially pp. 130–31.
14. G. Pettinato, *Das altorientalische Menschenbild und die sumerischen und akkadischen Schöpfungsmythen* (Heidelberg: Carl Winter, 1971), 31, 82–85.

Egyptians regarded the god who created the world as Atum. In one text, an early dedication ritual of a royal pyramid, the protection of the pyramid is compared to the creation of the world as a hill rising out of the water:

> Atum, you were high on the (first) hill. You arose (from the stone of the sacred sanctuary) as the sacred bird of the sacred stone in the sacred temple in Heliopolis. You spit out the god of air, you sputtered out the goddess of moisture. You put your arms about them. . . . So put your arms about this (dead) king, about this construction work, about this pyramid.[15]

Another early Egyptian reference to creation also makes explicit the connection with the creation of the cult. This reference comes from a set of instructions given by a ruler to his son about 2200 B.C.E., or more than fifteen hundred years earlier than the composition of Genesis 1:

> Well directed are men, the cattle of the god. He made heaven and earth according to their desire, and he repelled the water-monster. He made the breath of life for their nostrils. They who have issued from his body are his images. He arises in heaven according to their desire. He made for them plants, animals, fowl, and fish to feed them. He slew his enemies and injured his own children because they thought of making rebellion. He makes the light of day according to their desire. . . . *He has erected a shrine around them, and when they weep he hears.*[16]

The main creation texts, however, come from the primary cults of ancient Egypt, Memphis and Thebes. The earliest Egyptian cult center, or capital, was Memphis, the first city to rule over a united Upper and Lower Egypt. From Memphis came the conception of creation by the god Ptah through the act of thinking (a fitting conception for the rich). Ptah conceived of the world in his mind, then brought his conceptions into existence by his speech, much like God in Genesis 1, more than two thousand years later. The place of creation, Memphis, was presented as the "place where the two lands were united," and the temple of Ptah as the "balance in which Upper and

15. *ANET,* 3, with modifications.
16. *ANET,* 417.

Lower Egypt have been weighed."[17] It was Ptah who created even the great god Atum:

> There came into being as the heart and there came into being as the tongue (something) in the form of Atum. The mighty Great One is Ptah, who transmitted life to all gods, as well as to their vital force, through his mind, by which Horus became Ptah [i.e., Horus took on the attribute of thought] and through his tongue, by which Thoth became Ptah [took on the attribute of speech]. Thus it happened that the mind and tongue gained control over every other member of the body, by teaching that Ptah is in every body and in every mouth of all gods, all men, all cattle, all creeping things, and everything that lives, by thinking and commanding everything that he wishes. . . . It was said of Ptah, "He who made all and brought the gods into being." He is indeed the one who brought forth the gods, for everything came forth from him, nourishment and provisions, the offerings of the gods, and every good thing. . . . He had formed the gods, he had made cities, he had founded administrative districts, he had put the gods in their shrines, he had established their offerings, he had founded their shrines, he had made their bodies like what their minds would find satisfying. So the gods entered into their bodies of every kind of wood, stone, clay, or anything that might grow upon Ptah as the rising land.[18]

In this account of creation, the word of command plays the primary role, and attention is given to the creation, by command, of the districts of rule and administration, in which the various local gods, like so many administrators, take their seats, to be provisioned from local village produce. The command springing from mind and tongue may be primary, but of course some people's command was more primary than that of others. The primary command would stem from the ruler and priests of Memphis.

Later, during the New Kingdom period, a new capital with extensive temples was established at Thebes. In the view of the rulers of Thebes at that time, the primary command no longer emanated from Memphis or, for the period of this text, Amarna, but from Thebes, with its great temple at Karnak and associated shrines. The great god of Thebes was Amon-Re. One stanza from a twenty-eight-stanza set of poems on the city and its god runs as follows:

> More ordered is Thebes than any city. The water and land were in her from the beginning of time. Sand came to delimit (?) her fields

---

17. *ANET*, 4.
18. *ANET*, 4–6, excerpted and slightly modified.

and to create her ground on the (first) hill. Thus earth came into being. Then people came into being in her, to found every city in her real name, for they may be called "city" only under the oversight of Thebes, the Eye of Re. Her majesty came as the Sound Eye and the Beneficial Eye, to bind the land thereby together with her vital force, coming to rest and alighting in the sanctuary called Ishru, near Karnak, in her form as Sekhmet, the Mistress of the Two Lands. "How rich she is," they say about her, "in her name of Thebes."[19]

UGARIT

While many further examples of creation accounts and their relation to cults could be cited from the ancient Near East, it will be enough to give only one more, in some ways more closely related to the Bible than those already looked at. This account comes from the city of Ugarit, on the Mediterranean coast of what is today Syria, some two hundred miles north of Jerusalem, but in language and theme quite similar to much that is in the Bible. The Ugaritic myth of Baal is the story of how Baal's temple cult was founded, a temple and cult modeled on the palace of the king of Ugarit and its provision, which are similar to palaces and temples through the coastal areas of the eastern Mediterranean in ancient times.

The narrative of Baal opens with Baal's lord, the patriarchal El, sitting in his divine tent at the head of an assembly of gods. Messengers arrive from the god Yam, or Sea, analogous to Tiamat, demanding that El turn over Baal to Sea so that he can "assume his inheritance."[20] Should this occur, the principle of palace and dynastic rule for which Baal stands would not be established. Indeed, since crops cannot grow in sea-drenched land, it is not clear whether under Sea's rule there would be any prosperity at all, and whether Baal, who stands for the fructifying fresh waters of sky and rain, could establish the prosperity of the land. In the mercantile kingdom that was Ugarit, there must be room and importance given to local production.

The divine craftsman in Baal's entourage predicted Baal's victory:

Let me tell you, Prince Baal,

---

19. *ANET*, 8, with modifications.
20. Translations of the Baal narrative are taken from Michael David Coogan, *Stories from Ancient Canaan* (Philadelphia: Westminster Press, 1978), 86–115.

> Let me repeat, Rider on the Clouds:
> Behold, your enemy, Baal,
> > behold, you will kill your enemy,
> > behold, you will annihilate your foes.
> You will take your eternal kingship,
> > your dominion forever and ever.

Then the craftsman undertook to make Baal two magic clubs, called Driver and Chaser. "Driver, drive Sea from his throne; Chaser, chase Sea from his throne." With these Baal killed Sea. Now young Baal wanted his own house. With other gods lobbying for him, he finally persuaded El to allow him to have his own house built. Once again the craftsman went into action. He produced abundant works of gold, silver, and valuable woods: canopies, couches, a spendid platform and throne, tables, and utensils. When the temple was finished:

> Baal the conqueror was glad:
> "I have built my house of silver,
> > my palace of gold."
> Baal prepared the house,
> > Hadad [Baal] made preparations within his palace:
> he slaughtered oxen,
> > he killed sheep,
> > bulls, fatling rams,
> > yearling calves;
> he strangled lambs and kids.
> He invited his brothers into his house,
> > his cousins within his palace;
> > he invited Asherah's seventy sons.
> He gave the gods lambs;
> > he gave the gods ewes;
> > he gave the gods oxen;
> > he gave the gods seats;
> > he gave the gods thrones;
> he gave the gods a jar of wine;
> > he gave the goddesses a cask of wine.
> Until the gods had eaten and drunk their fill,
> > he gave them sucklings to eat,
> > with a sharp knife carved the breast of a fatling.
> They drank wine from goblets,
> > blood of the vine from golden cups. . . .
> Baal captured sixty-six cities,

seventy-seven towns;
Baal sacked eighty,
    Baal sacked ninety;
then Baal returned to his house.

Baal instituted the feeding of the gods that would later be carried out in the cult of the king of Ugarit. On the basis of this provision, he went out to capture a hundred towns and villages, and their village workers, over whom the king of Ugarit would rule and from whose produce he would prosper.

It is not surprising that creation texts should have so much to do with the cults of ancient cities. Creation is an activity or function of the gods. Creation means in essence that the world as known was produced by a god. As the cult presents itself as the location and occasion for meeting or serving the god, and hence at the center of the world produced by the god, the narrative of world production called "creation" naturally finds its place in the cult. The same is true of the Bible.

2

More Than One
Creation Story

For many people it comes as a surprise to find out that Genesis 1 is not the only account of creation in the Bible. There are many accounts of creation in the Bible. Genesis 1 is not *the* creation account, merely a creation account. It is the most famous only because it comes at the beginning of the Bible. It is not, however, the oldest account in the Bible by any means, nor does it represent the commonest view of creation in the Bible.

EXODUS

The earliest reference to creation in the Bible is found in Exodus 15:1–18, a song celebrating victory in battle, from all indications composed in its present form some time before, or possibly during, the reign of David in the tenth century B.C.E. This song is typical of biblical accounts of creation in three important ways. First, creation is understood explicitly to refer to creation of a world for a particular community or society. Second, creation is expressed especially in terms of God's defeat of the waters of the sea or God's control over those waters. Third, the account ties creation to the focus of the particular community in its cult.

> Pharaoh's chariots and his army God has cast into the sea,
>   and his officers are sunk in the Sup Sea.
> The floods cover them;
>   they went down into the depths like a stone.
> At the blast of your nostrils the waters piled up,

19

the floods stood up in a heap;
the deeps congealed in the heart of the sea.
You blew with your wind, the sea covered them;
they sank as lead in the mighty waters.

The poem goes on to describe the passage, in procession, of the people rescued or "redeemed" by this action of God. The kings and chiefs of the surrounding states are seized with dread at this people and the protection they receive from their God,

Until your people, Yahweh, pass by,
until the people pass by whom you have created.

The term rendered "created" here rather than "purchased" as in the RSV is the same term used to describe God as the creator of heavens and earth in Genesis 14:19, 22. As in practically all creation accounts in the Bible, this earliest one ties creation to the cult:

You will bring them in, and plant them on your conquered
mountain,
the shrine, Yahweh, which you have made for your abode,
the sanctuary, Yahweh, which your hands have established.

Like other ancient Near Eastern creation accounts, this account is part of a longer narrative that helps to establish a cult of sacrifice in a capital city, under royal dominion. It was incorporated into the Bible's first history during the period of David. It represents the attempt of David's scribe to put the relatively modest tent cult of David, especially his cult in Jerusalem and his pilgrimage cult in the Sinai desert, in the context of the traditions of the seminomadic herdsmen who frequented his court and were supporters of his rule.[1]

THE TEMPLE

Although David was not in a position to build a proper temple for Yahweh, his son Solomon was. Solomon's temple, the chapel of the ruling dynasty of the house of David, was modeled on the typical dynastic temple of the eastern Mediterranean area. The conception of God that it represented was close to that of Baal in the Ugaritic myth of Baal. Solomon brought a master craftsman in bronze from Tyre to oversee the crafting of bronze utensils and accessories for the temple.

1. See Robert B. Coote and David R. Ord, *The Bible's First History* (Minneapolis: Fortress Press, 1989).

Included among these was a huge bronze basin for holding water to model the sea, placed within the temple:

> Then he made the molten sea; it was round, ten cubits from brim to brim, and five cubits high, and a line of thirty cubits measured its circumference. Under its brim were gourds, for thirty cubits, compassing the sea round about; the gourds were in two rows, cast with it when it was cast. It stood upon twelve oxen, three facing north, three west, three south, and three east. The sea was set upon them, and all their hinder parts were inward. Its thickness was a handbreadth; and its brim was made like the brim of a cup, like the flower of a lily; it held two thousand baths of water. (1 Kings 7:23-26, RSV)[2]

In the conception of the cult of the royal temple, this was the sea that Yahweh defeated in battle just as did Baal. This is described in Psalm 29, itself a hymn to Baal simply adopted for the praise of Yahweh by replacing the name Baal with Yahweh:

> The voice of Yahweh is against the waters;
>   the God of glory thunders,
>   Yahweh, against many waters.
> The voice of Yahweh is powerful,
>   the voice of Yahweh is full of majesty. . . .
> Yahweh sits enthroned over the flood;
>   Yahweh sits enthroned as king for ever.

This conception of Yahweh's victory over the raging waters of the sea, the same as the god Sea at Ugarit or Tiamat at Babylon, is celebrated in a number of other compositions in the Bible. These include Psalms 93 and 95–99. In all of these, the creation of the cult is tantamount to the creation of the world, since for all of them the defeat of Sea is a prerequisite for creation.

Sea in the Bible is often portrayed as the dragon or monster, as in the Babylonian and Ugaritic texts. Sometimes the same term is used. In its vision of the re-creation of the city and cult, Isaiah 27:1 uses the same name and epithet for sea that occurs in one Ugaritic text:

> In that day Yahweh with his hard and great and strong sword will punish Leviathan the fleeing serpent, and he will slay the dragon that is in the sea.

---

2. Throughout this book, translations from *The Revised Standard Version* are marked RSV, and those from *The New American Bible* (New York: P.J. Kenedy and Sons, 1970) are marked NAB. Any Bible quotations not marked RSV or NAB are translations by the authors.

Another name for this monster was Rahab, the "great" one. In an allusion to the same event, Job commented:

> God will not turn back his anger;
>   beneath him bowed the helpers of Rahab. (Job 9:13, RSV)

And similarly:

> By his power he stilled the sea;
>   by his understanding he smote Rahab.
> By his wind the heavens were made fair;
>   his hand pierced the fleeing serpent. (Job 26:12-13)

Likewise, in the long description of Yahweh's actions of creation at the end of Job, Yahweh says:

> Where were you when I laid the foundation of the earth? (Job 38:4)
> Can you draw out Leviathan with a fishhook,
>   or press down his tongue with a cord? (Job 41:1)

There follows a full description of Yahweh's defeat of this sea dragon in the act of creation.

SECOND ISAIAH AND EXILE

In the sixth century B.C.E., Second Isaiah[3] foresaw the reestablishment of the royal cult of Jerusalem as a repeat of a similar creation:

> Awake, awake, put on strength,
>   O arm of Yahweh;
> awake, as in days of old,
>   the generations of long ago.
> Was it not you that bored Rahab,
>   that pierced the dragon?
> Was it not you that dried up the sea,
>   the waters of the great deep;[4]
> that made the depths of the sea a way
>   for the redeemed to pass over?
> The ransomed of Yahweh shall return,
>   and come with singing to Zion. (Isa. 51:9-11)

---

3. Second Isaiah is the way historians refer to the part of the book of Isaiah written not by the eighth-century prophet of Jerusalem named Isaiah, who composed much of what appears in Isaiah 1–33, but by a prophetic Judahite poet resident in Babylon around 539 B.C.E., whose name is not known because his work was presented as though composed by Isaiah. It consists of Isaiah 40–55, and possibly 34–35.
4. Hebrew *tehom*, cognate with Babylonian *Tiamat*.

There are a number of similar descriptions, especially in the psalms, that lament the violation and destruction of the royal cult of Jerusalem in the sixth century B.C.E.:

> When the waters saw you, O God,
>> when the waters saw you, they were afraid,
>> yea, the deep trembled.
> The clouds poured out water;
>> the skies gave forth thunder;
>> your arrows flashed on every side.
> The crash of your thunder was in the whirlwind;
>> your lightnings lighted up the world;
>> the earth trembled and shook.
> Your way was through the sea,
>> your path through the great waters;
>> yet your footprints were unseen.
> You led your people like a flock
>> by the hand of Moses and Aaron. (Ps. 77:16-20).

> You divided the sea by your might;
>> you broke the heads of the dragons over the waters.
> You crushed the heads of Leviathan,
>> you gave him as food . . .
> You cleaved open springs and wadies,
>> you dried up steadily flowing rivers.
> Yours is the day, yours also the night;
>> you founded the luminaries of the sky and the sun.
> You fixed all the bounds of the earth;
>> you made late summer and early fall. (Ps. 74:13-17)

Note how in this latter account the defeat of sea for the cult precedes the global elements of creation. The last line refers not simply to the ordering of the seasons, but specifically to the organization of dry and rainy seasons, with their boundary usually in September in Palestine.

Another example occurs in Psalm 89:

> Let the sky praise your wonders, Yahweh,
>> your truth in the assembly of the divine holy ones.
> You rule the raging of the sea;
>> when its waves rise, you still them.
> You crushed Rahab like a carcass,
>> you scattered your enemies with your mighty arm.

The heavens are yours, the earth also yours;
  the earth and all that is in it, you founded them. (vv. 5, 9-11)

These words are the prelude in Psalm 89 to the singer's plea for God's mercy toward the afflicted house of David, and by inference toward the temple cult it established and maintained for four hundred years prior to the time this song was composed. Yahweh goes on to promise:

Once for all I have sworn by my holiness;
  I will not lie to David.
His line shall endure for ever,
  his throne as long as the sun before me.
Like the moon it shall be established for ever;
  it is a witness as sure as the sky. (vv. 35-37).

JEREMIAH AND AMOS

The stability of the house of David is secured by the stability of creation itself. This idea is similar to the references to creation in Jeremiah 31:35–37 and 33:19–22, in which the account of creation implied is quite close to Genesis 1:

Thus says Yahweh,
  who gives the sun for light by day
  and the fixed order of the moon
  and the stars for light by night,
who stirs up the sea so that its waves roar—
  Yahweh of hosts is his name:
"If this fixed order departs
  from before me," says Yahweh,
"Then shall the descendants of Israel cease
  from being a nation before me for ever."

Thus says Yahweh,
"If the heavens above can be measured,
  and the foundations of the earth below can be explored,
then I will cast off all the descendants of Israel
  for all that they have done," says Yahweh.

The word of Yahweh came to Jeremiah: "Thus says Yahweh: If you can break my covenant with the day and my covenant with the night, so that day and night will not come at their appointed time, then also my covenant with David my servant may be broken, so that he shall not have a son to reign on his throne. . . . As the host of heaven cannot be numbered and the sands of the sea cannot be measured, so I will multiply the descendants of David my servant."

Similar images are employed in the book of Amos, probably in reference to Jerusalem once again, in the seventh century B.C.E. edition of the words of Amos:[5]

The one who forms the mountains,
    and creates the wind,
and declares to humans their thoughts,
    who makes the morning darkness,
    and treads on the heights of the earth—
Yahweh the god of armed hosts is his name. (Amos 4:13)

He who made the Pleiades and Orion,
    and turns deep darkness into the morning,
    and darkens day into night,
who calls for the waters of the sea,
    and pours them out upon the surface of the earth,
Yahweh is his name. (Amos 5:8)

The creation restored could be the creation reversed as well. The vision of Jeremiah 4:23-26 sees world order turned into chaos, as Yahweh's response to present injustice:

I looked at the earth, and behold it was waste,
    at the heavens, and there was no light.
I beheld the mountains, and behold they trembled,
    and all the hills heaved to and fro.
I looked and behold, humanity was naught,
    and the birds of the sky had flown.

5. This edition is known as Amos B. Like nearly all of the Bible, the book of Amos was written over a period of time, even though most of what is in it may go back to the prophet Amos, who lived in the eighth century B.C.E. Different parts of the book of Amos are written in such a way as to reflect the interests of different times and places. Amos A is a way of referring to the speeches in the book of Amos that denounce the ruling class of eighth-century Samaria. Amos B refers to speeches and incidents related to the Israelite cult at Bethel, north of Jerusalem. These speeches and incidents were partly composed by Amos, and partly written by seventh-century scribes in Jerusalem. They have been included in the book of Amos to reflect not only Amos's concern, but also the hostility of the rulers of Jerusalem toward Bethel during the seventh century, especially in the time of Josiah in the last quarter of the century. See Robert B. Coote, *Amos Among the Prophets* (Philadelphia: Fortress Press, 1981). For a contrary view, see Max E. Polley, *Amos and the Davidic Empire: A Socio-historical Approach* (New York: Oxford University Press, 1989).

I looked, and behold, the tilled land was steppe,
   and all its cities ruins;
because of Yahweh,
   because of his burning wrath.[6]

OTHER PSALMS

There are at least two other conceptions of the cult that use such
imagery of creation in their representation of the cult and the social
order at whose center it stands. One of these is that of the cult as the
focal point of jurisdiction. Psalm 24 is representative of this conception:

> The earth is Yahweh's, and everything that fills it,
>   the world and those who inhabit it;
> for he has founded it upon the seas,
>   and established it upon the rivers.
> Who shall ascend the hill of Yahweh?
>   And who shall stand in his holy shrine?

The answer given is that the person who guards fair and true witness
and judgment in the adjudication of particular cases is the one to be
admitted to God's cult.

   The other conception is the cult as the place where a select priesthood carry out the services of feeding God and themselves as God's
representatives. This conception is delineated in Psalm 8, which de-
picts both the way the priests of Solomon's temple thought of themselves, and also the way their much later heirs, the writers of Genesis
1, portrayed humanity:

> Yahweh our lord,
>   how majestic is your name in all the earth,
>   . . . splendor above the sky.
> Apart from the voices of babies and sucklings[7]
>   you founded strength,
> Because of your adversaries,
>   to put to nothing the victorious enemy.
> When I see your sky,
>   the work of your fingers,
>   the moon and stars you established,

6. This translation is from Michael Fishbane, "Jeremiah IV 23–26 and Job III 3-13: A Recovered
Use of the Creation Pattern," *Vetus Testamentum* 21 (1971): 151–67.
7. That is, before human beings were present, before God had yet created human beings.

> What is a man that you recall him,
>> A human, that you take note of him?
> You have made him less than God by only a bit;
>> with glory and honor you have crowned him.
> You have given him rule over the work of your hands;
>> You have placed all beneath his feet—
> All flocks of sheep, herds of cattle,
>> Even the beasts of the open country,
> Birds of the sky and fish of the sea,
>> Everything that makes its path in the sea.
> Yahweh our lord,
>> how majestic is your name in all the earth.

This concept of humans as only a bit less than God comes from the elite priesthood of the capital. Priests sacrificed the animals of the cult and lived as though they were gods.

Still other conceptions of God's creation have found their way into the hymnal of the cult of the Persian and Hellenistic period temple in Jerusalem. Psalm 104 outlines the created order in detail, and it is an order that differs considerably from Genesis 1. In this account animals and humans are already in existence as the earth takes shape and plants begin to appear. Psalm 136 parallels the creation of the world with the creation of God's people in the way we have just seen in several examples. Its account of the creation of the world runs as follows, omitting the psalm's refrain:

> To him who by understanding made the sky,
>> to him who spread out the earth upon the waters,
>> to him who made the great lights,
>> the sun to rule over the day,
>> the moon and stars to rule over the night.

In at least two other psalms, the priestly concept of the creative fiat, or word of creation, appears:

> By the word of Yahweh the sky was made,
>> and all their host by the breath of his mouth.
> He gathers the waters of the sea as in a bottle;
>> he puts the deeps in storehouses. (Ps. 33:6-7)

Note again the different order of creation implied by this citation from the other psalm using this conception:

> Praise Yahweh, sun and moon,

praise him, all you shining stars.
Praise him, you highest heavens,
    and you waters above the heavens.
Let them praise the name of Yahweh,
    for he commanded and they were created.
And he established them for ever and ever;
    he fixed their bounds which cannot be passed.
Praise Yahweh from the earth,
    you sea monsters and all deeps,
fire and hail, snow and frost,[8]
    stormy wind fulfilling his command.
Mountains and all hills,
    fruit trees and all cedars.
Beasts and all cattle,
    creeping things and flying birds.
Kings of the earth and all courts,
    princes and all rulers of the earth.
Young men and maidens together,
    old men and children. (Ps. 148:3-12)

As just one account of creation among many in the Old Testament, Genesis 1 is not even particularly typical. It makes only weak allusion to the control of the cosmic waters, especially in the sense of the aggressive and opposing sea, which Yahweh subdues in his military majesty as the cult of the king and his temple are established. Even in as clear an apparent allusion to Genesis as can be supposed in Nehemiah 9:6, a different order of elements can be discerned. Here the order is sky, earth, water, instead of sky, water, earth, as in Genesis 1:

> You are Yahweh, you alone. You made heaven, the heaven of heavens, with all their host, the earth and all that is on it, the seas and all that is in them. And you preserve all of them.

It is apparent, then, that the order of elements in Genesis 1 serves a particular purpose in terms of the larger literary and historical context from which it comes. We turn now to the question of what that context is. Who wrote Genesis 1, and why?

---

8. Hail, snow, and frost are derived from the cosmic deeps.

3

Who Wrote
Genesis One?

Who created the creation story of Genesis 1? Although Genesis, Exodus, Leviticus, Numbers, and Deuteronomy may pretend to have been composed prior to the founding of the Davidic kingdom, in their earliest form the traditions were not arranged as the five books with which we are familiar. What appears as a single narrative is in reality a composite intertwining of four main narratives,[1] composed at different times. Because we do not know the names of those who composed the four literary works that form the basis of the first five books of the Bible, they are commonly referred to by the letters J, E, D, and P.

THE PENTATEUCH

These four narratives arose at times of crisis in Israel's history. Each of them is a fresh articulation of the worldview of a particular group of Israelites (never all Israelites) to meet the needs of their changed circumstances. Each consists of a legitimating history of cult, composed for successive rulers or ruling groups at the start of their rule. J was composed when David usurped the Israelite state. In the course of the history of monarchic Israel, this document underwent periodic recomposition. E and P, which may never have been complete works on their own, came into being as supplementary revisions of J. The creation story of Genesis 1 is the beginning of P, whereas the creation story that begins in Genesis 2:4b is the beginning of J. D is a complete story, although the part contained in the Pentateuch, mostly in the

---

1. Scholars speak of the narratives as strands, or sources.

book of Deuteronomy, is only the beginning of its story, which continues all the way through the books of Kings. The end result of this process of recomposition is known to us as the Pentateuch and Former Prophets, or the books of Genesis through 2 Kings (excepting Ruth, which comes much later in the Hebrew Bible).

Since the Bible came into being through a lengthy and complex process of writing spanning a thousand years or more, it represents the experiences of forty or fifty generations with scores of thousands of people in each generation. Not only did each generation's experiences differ, but also even within the space of a generation there were frequent and basic disagreements about power, rights, and the way the world works. For instance, if one were a peasant, one's view of the created order and one's place in that order were different from those held by the political and social elite. Most peasants probably believed themselves to have been created to serve their rulers, but may also have considered rulers to be oppressors and perpetrators of injustice. Rulers, on the other hand, tended to see their superior social standing as a God-given right, judging from the literature they have left us.

To answer the question of who created the creation story of Genesis 1, we must know which generation it comes from and whose views and rights it represents.

PRIESTS OF THE ELITE

Although writing as we know it dates back about five thousand years, it was not commonplace. Even rulers had to rely heavily on scribes, who were practically the only literate people in the realm. These scribes were generally the clerical wing of the priesthood of the realm. Priests played a cardinal role in the establishment and maintenance of the state.

By fostering fear of the god among the peasantry who formed the bulk of the population, temples in ancient times functioned as a source of law and order in society and were supported as such particularly by those who enjoyed the benefits of ostensible social order. Throughout the Near East, rulers endorsed and were endorsed by endowed temple organizations run by hereditary priestly families. These organizations backed up the legitimacy of the ruling family and the ruling class. The priesthood was thus closely connected to the state. The priests were members of the ruling class. In fact, priestly and political hierarchies were often nearly indistinguishable, as was the case in Palestine when the temple priests of Jerusalem became the primary on-site rulers of Judah in the Persian period.

The priests in charge of a temple received not only large returns from the villages on the lands whose tenure they held, together with other receipts in the form of taxes enforced by the ruler, but also contributions in kind in the form of sacrifices. The state shrine was a cult of meat sacrifice.[2] It was a primary privilege of the priesthood as a class to eat meat in abundance, and during some periods even to claim the privilege of having no meat slaughtered in the realm at all except under their supervision and participation—a prerogative impossible to enforce. Sacrifices were essentially tribute, to both the officeholders themselves and to the organization of the temple and the political and legal arrangements it sanctioned and fostered. The emphasis on sheep sacrifice in Israel's temple cult is probably a reflection of Jerusalem's location near the border zones of Palestine, where sheep and goats were always a significant component of local agriculture. Male sheep were sacrificed, and female sheep were kept, because one male can impregnate a lot of females. But a male sacrifice had to be a good sheep, not a poor one, since it was to provision the priestly class.[3]

State cults of sacrifice required full-time specialists. The priesthood was thus professional. A temple's cult of the priestly meal of sacrifices combined with priestly land tenure to free its guardian priesthood and assistants from the need to earn their living in other pursuits, in order that they might pursue their duties as butchers of sacrifices, cult petitioners, taboo specialists, artists, scribes, lawyers, judges, counselors, prophets, and warriors. What gave these many roles their coherence, so that it was possible to refer to the practitioners with the single word priest, was the shrine and its rites. In Palestine, the institution lasted for over a thousand years, with many historical changes in the basic pattern of priestly privileges and responsibilities.

In the Mediterranean world, there were many shrines at different levels of jurisdiction, but the most important one was the state capital

---

2. There were also grain offerings, but meat offerings were the salient feature of the cult.

3. "In the overfed West we can easily fail to realize what was involved in offering an unblemished animal in sacrifice. Meat was a rare luxury in Old Testament times for all but the very rich. Yet even we might blanch if we saw a whole lamb or bull go up in smoke as a burnt offering. How much greater pangs must a poor Israelite have felt" (Gordon J. Wenham, *The Book of Leviticus* [Grand Rapids, Eerdmans, 1979], 51).

shrine. The shrines of Palestine were tended by several significant priestly groups during the biblical period, but the clearest example was the priesthood of the temple of the house of David in Jerusalem. The priestly caste of biblical Palestine would not have viewed themselves simply as just another part of the ruling class. They wished to magnify their distinctiveness over against other elites. Thus the detailed description of the elaborate priestly cult of which Genesis 1 is the basis has the purpose not so much of differentiating the priests from the laity, but from other elites.

Like most priesthoods in the ancient world, the Jerusalem priesthood embraced an important clerical element. The Bible comes almost entirely from the clerical element of the Jerusalem priesthood, which makes this priesthood of particular interest to us. While there are many gaps and uncertainties in our understanding of the history of this priesthood, its broad outlines can be described as follows.

PRIESTS OF THE HOUSE OF DAVID

David, under whose rule the state of Israel was fully organized, apparently supported two priestly groups, which may have been in competition, represented by Abiathar and Zadok. Abiathar came from Shiloh and traced his ancestry theoretically back to Moses. Zadok, whom David appointed as his own family priest, came from Judah and was closely associated with families tied to David in his rise to power. The heirs of Zadok traced their ancestry back to Aaron.

Moses and Aaron both had Egyptian names. Both were apparently of the priestly house of Levi, in which there were other Egyptian names. This old, large family was established during the period of the Egyptian New Kingdom's sovereignty over Palestine. As Egyptian power receded and independent villages and agriculture became established in the Palestine highlands, various branches of the family retained their priestly prerogatives in the different localities that were to become the birthplace of the biblical state of Israel. When David came to power, he drew on the support of the Levites and accepted and fostered the authority of Moses, to the point of promulgating his modest cult law in the name of Moses. Moses appears to have been the dominant figure in the family at one time, the man who possessed the bulk of power and prestige in the family's remembrance.

When Solomon succeeded David with the support of private palace forces in contrast to popular forces, he established the priesthood that was to service the temple he had constructed by ousting the representative of wide Levite support, Abiathar, and installing Zadok as sole chief priest. The house of Zadok claimed Levite descent through Aaron. It could not, however, recover the popular and broad backing of the Levites at large, who continued serving as priests throughout the land as they had in David's time and before. They were especially important in the traditional shrine of Shiloh in the northern hill country.

While Moses remained important to the royal house down through the years, Aaron came to be regarded as the special ancestor and patron of the temple priesthood. There may also have been Aaronid priests in Bethel during the existence of the northern kingdom of Israel. The Zadokite priests of the temple in Jerusalem were thus in theory a special branch of those Levites who served throughout the land and who increasingly regarded themselves as disadvantaged in relation to the privileged Zadokites.

As a result of their privileged position, the Zadokites became a powerful family in Judah, and their power and privilege lasted for centuries. The traditions of this dominant priestly family grew up in the time of Solomon with their early role in the lavish rites of the temple that formed the royal chapel. There were ups and downs, depending among other things on the relative importance of the temple itself in a particular period, but the family persisted as one of the most powerful in the realm. They were a dominant ruling elite from the time of David throughout the earlier biblical period.

The Zadokites were strongly confirmed in particular in the time of Hezekiah, who removed from the temple the bronze snake, an icon associated with the authority of Moses. Under Hezekiah's temple reform, all priestly rites had to be performed in Jerusalem. Such a restriction was possible for the first time in Israel only under Hezekiah and greatly limited the influence of priests outside Jerusalem. Hezekiah's territory had been considerably reduced under pressure from Assyria, and his strong support for the Zadokites reflects his interest in consolidating his power within the narrow confines left to his sovereignty, which may have included little more than an enlarged Jerusalem and its immediate environs toward Hebron. Even though the resource base of the temple had shrunk significantly, the temple priesthood benefited from Hezekiah's program; for whenever the resources of the temple shrank, the Aaronid Zadokites claimed their special privilege, and the other Levites of the land suffered in consequence.

A century after Hezekiah, Josiah foresaw new sources of wealth for the state as the result of the ebbing of Assyrian power and his own campaigns of conquest. In his attempt to restore the sovereignty and prestige of the house of David not only in Judah but elsewhere in Israelite Palestine, it is likely that he had the support of Egypt. Although in the end he rebelled against Egypt, his supporting faction was associated with Egypt, as well as with the successor power in Palestine, Babylon. During the period of Assyrian threat, the Zadokites had been somewhat compromised by their collusion with the occupying Assyrians. They had gained personal power through the diminished power and prestige of the house of David. In his bid to gain popularity in order to oppose the Assyrians, Josiah climbed to power not on the ladder of the Zadokites but of the other Levite families of the land. He partially succeeded, through both military campaign and the support of a faction including Hilkiah, Shaphan, and Jeremiah. These represented a tradition going back to Shiloh and regarded Moses and Samuel as greater authorities than Aaron. Josiah imposed a centralization similar to Hezekiah's, but the Levites were not to be excluded from the privileges of priestly service in Jerusalem. In Josiah's temple priestly arrangement, the Levites took up the roles they were to play in the temple for several centuries to come, as assistants, servants, clerks, scribes, and the like—for the most part, services ancillary to the main cult of meat sacrifice.

Josiah had a great law collection and history composed, known now as the Deuteronomistic history. It represents a sophisticated amalgam of Moses and David traditions. D is Josiah's law collection and history.

Babylonians invaded Judah in 605 B.C.E., 604, and 598. In 598 B.C.E. they deported the bulk of the house of David and put their own puppet on the Davidic throne. Eleven years later they destroyed the temple altogether. The Zadokites of the late Davidic monarchy suffered severe cruelty and deprivation under Babylonian control. The chief members of the families were executed, and hundreds of others deported to Babylon. Ezekiel is a representative of their number.

During the period of Babylonian rule in Palestine, the Levite groups that had supported Josiah were pro-Babylonian. Their views and expectations are contained in writings like the Deuteronomistic history, the book of Jeremiah, and the Deuteronomistic recompositions of Amos and Micah.

THE PERSIAN PERIOD

When the Persian ruling class came to power in Babylon, they were looking for loyal descendants of the elite families that headed the state of Judah two generations earlier. At first they were willing to send back members of the royal house of David itself, including Sheshbazzar and Zerubbabel, both of whom were appointed governors. But upon the accession of Darius over the Persian Empire, the Davidic royal house soon disappeared altogether—in all likelihood because Persia could not permit the sovereignty of a king, and because the house of David had such a significant component that acquiesced to the power of Babylon, as is so eloquently expressed in Jeremiah. In the wake of the demise of the royal house, the Zadokite priestly families again came into their own.

When the building of a new temple and favorable Persian administrative policy led to the reempowerment of a surviving sector of the Aaronid Zadokites, Josiah's faction lost out. The Zadokites were restored as the recipients of the temple taxes and tribute sacrifices. They again became the chief landholders in Persian-controlled Palestine, probably falling back on recovered traditional land holdings and patronage positions over the local population. They became a new ruling elite, only this time without the house of David around to keep their power in check, in effect a surrogate royalty. A third governor, apparently not of the royal family, Elnathan, in the late sixth century B.C.E. married a Davidic princess because the power even of the governorship was falling in relation to the power of the chief priest, Yeshua at the time. The increasing power of the restored Zadokite priesthood is also indicated by Yeshua's title—high priest instead of chief priest—which indicates that he held additional and important administrative responsibilities.

The Zadokite priesthood did not require the house of David for its own success, especially not under the Persians. They were a clergy, or clerisy, assuming for themselves the prerogatives of cultural centralization for the people in their charge:

> The cognitive centralization and codification effected by a clerisy, and the political centralization which is the state, need not go hand

in hand. Often they are rivals; sometimes one may capture the
other; but more often . . . the specialists of violence and of faith
are indeed independently operating rivals, and their territories are
often not coextensive. . . . Of the two potential partners, culture
and power [as the force of the state] . . . neither has much inclination
for the other in the conditions prevailing in the agrarian age.[4]

The authority of the Zadokites was exercised through the customs,
taboos, and laws they inherited from their forebears of the monarchic
period. For a hundred years the temple scriptures had been under the
control of the Mosaic and Levitical scribes established by Josiah, but
they were now back in the hands of the Zadokites. All the writings
of Josiah's faction were relegated to the second rank of scripture, where
they remain today (the Prophets), a sign of their secondary authority
among the loose scrolls of the temple scriptures under the Zadokites.
Primary place went to the views and perspectives of the Zadokite
group, supported by the Persians, and this is what we have now in
the priestly history that organizes the priestly version of the first four
books of the Bible. The priestly history is the literary form in which
these views and perspectives were made an integral part of the monarchic period temple scriptures.

But the Levites continued to hold important ancillary functions in
the temple complex, as described in the books of Chronicles and seen
in the Levitical portions of the Psalms. These included continued
scribal service, so that while some parts of scripture did represent the
Aaronid Zadokite point of view, the Levitical view continued to get
a hearing, especially when it was closer to the Persian view than that
of the Aaronids themselves. A good example of Levitical influence
in the continuing production of temple scripture is the case of Isaiah.

Under the rule of the Zadokite temple priests, the temple, which
had been rebuilt under Persian auspices, came on hard times. This
rebuilt temple was never an impressive institution, either in terms of
the quality of its structure, or in terms of the scope of its influence.
Its agricultural base was much reduced from its great days in the reigns
of Solomon, Jehoshaphat, Uzziah, and Josiah. Despite this, the authority of its Zadokite law was widely imposed, at least nominally,
as it was on its basis that the Persian sovereigns were happy to have
a compliant Palestine under their rule.

4. Ernst Gellner, *Nations and Nationalism* (Ithaca: Cornell University Press, 1983), 8–9, 11.

As trade was reestablished in the Mediterranean along a northeast-southwest axis through lowland Palestine, largely bypassing Persian control, the priestly families turned more and more to their own interests. Those responsible for maintaining Persian authority in Palestine came to betray Persian interests, as well as the interests of the Palestinian villagers under their jurisdiction, by joining lowland and dryland families participating in trade along mainly Greek-controlled routes. The Aaronid priests put their private family interests ahead of their temple interests and used the temple as a means of personal gain to the detriment of the temple. By the middle of the fifth century B.C.E., the Zadokites had become again like the Zadokites of the mid-seventh century: a strong nobility covertly opposed to royalty, supported but factionalized by outside powers—Assyria in the seventh century, mainly Greece now. Persian authority exercised chiefly through the temple was becoming little more than theoretical.

Under these circumstances the lesser priestly families of the temple—those identified as the Levites—came to suffer acutely. Consequently they began to pay even closer attention to the laws of the Torah, which they associated primarily with Moses and the Zadokites associated primarily with Aaron. Their complaints are voiced in Isaiah 56–66, where they claim to represent the full keeping of the laws of Moses over against the Zadokites, whom they accuse of following mainly the symbolic figure Abraham and his interest in circumcision. (Abraham would probably stand for the trading peoples of the south and west. The Zadokites saw their interest symbolized by Abraham because they were the beneficiaries of the trade to the south and west, which was not controlled by the Persians.) These lesser priests envisioned a new wealth flowing to the temple itself, rather than away from it, if the just laws of the Aaronid Torah, the primary temple scrolls authorized by the Zadokites themselves, were actually enforced—including of course a just provision for the Levites as described in Deuteronomy, which by now had been incorporated into the Torah.

The interests of these Levites coincided perfectly with the interests of the Persians, who also wanted to reduce the power of this growing force of local nobles and to increase the wealth and prestige of the temple, the focus of their own authority in Palestine and the center through which tribute flowed to Persia. They sent a strong Aaronid scribe loyal to the Persian court, Ezra. He attempted to break up local marriages between the Judahite nobility, including local Aaronids, and

Greek-connected lowland families. He also attempted to reconfirm the Aaronid law conveyed by Moses, including the Mosaic portions of the Deuteronomistic history (the book of Deuteronomy), to gain the support of the local Levites for his program. The Levites' vision as seen in Isaiah 56–66 was also backed by Nehemiah, whom the Persians sent as governor in mid-century. All this represented a renewed attempt on Persia's part to break the power of the combined forces of local priests, Greek elements, and "Abrahamic" elements or nomads to the south who were controlling Palestinian trade to the detriment of the Persians.

The entrenched priestly families of the Davidic temple in Jerusalem continued in varying power throughout the period of the temple. It is their scriptures we have in the Old Testament. The priestly history (P) was a written form of the traditions and laws of the Zadokites who came into power in the late sixth century under Persian sponsorship. It was they who composed the creation story of Genesis 1. The primacy of the priestly work is a function of the Persian policy to resurrect the temple priesthood in Palestine with the deepest roots and strongest patronage role based on highly persistent landholding patterns, going back ultimately to Solomon.

4

Revising the
Official History

The Zadokite Aaronid Jerusalemite priests of the middle to late sixth century B.C.E. recorded their traditions and laws in the form known to us today as the priestly history that organizes the Tetrateuch. We refer to both the writer and the work itself as P. Whether P was an individual or a committee has no bearing on its meaning. The priestly history appears in certain passages in Genesis and Exodus, virtually the whole of Leviticus (including what scholars call the Holiness Code in Leviticus 17-25), and about three-fourths of Numbers. The scrolls of the Torah were sponsored in their present form by the Aaronids. The scrolls of the prophets are mainly from the Levites, excepting Ezekiel, which is odd in more ways than one. The priestly history, beginning as it does with Genesis 1, represents the prerogatives of the temple Aaronids.

To understand the priestly work, in particular its creation account, it is not essential to decide whether it was written during the exile of important Zadokite families in Babylon before the Persian takeover, or after the Persian takeover, in Babylon or Jerusalem, as part of the restoration of the Davidic temple and its scriptural norms.[1]

---

1. It is easy to see Ezekiel, who like the priestly writer concerned himself with the restoration of the priestly cult, in the context of the Davidic court in exile in Babylon. Ezekiel refers and alludes often to the house of David. The priestly writer on the other hand never mentions David and makes little of either kings or monarchy (Gen. 17:6, 16; 35:11). The priestly writer anticipates the restoration of the former monarchic temple but mutes the monarchic implications of such a restoration. This may mean that the priestly history belongs to the period of Persian rule after the exile, before or after the rebuilding of the temple in 520–15, when the Aaronids themselves assumed the royal prerogatives of the capital but fell short of monarchic autonomy. The kings of Babylon had sponsored the scribal, sacerdotal activity of the Davidic court in exile, even

USE OF JE

It is essential to understand that the priestly writer did not compose his traditions in a vacuum. Whether in Babylon or Jerusalem, he inherited and had access to the official Jerusalemite history of the world, which made the cult of Yahweh the center of the world, and which came from the earlier Aaronid temple. This history, begun with a document called by scholars J and incorporating a revision called E, is often referred to by them as JE. The priestly writer used this history as his base.[2] Whether the priestly history once stood alone, or was from the first a revision of the official history, cannot be determined and is of little consequence.[3]

The priestly writer's use of the Davidic state history must be seen against the background of the question of Jerusalem temple loyalties toward the end of the sixth century B.C.E. The official history purported to tell the story of the first twenty-two generations of humanity. God was said to have brought the members of the nation of Israel together, and the motif of Egypt as a common enemy was employed to solidify the union. This basic theme was favorable to

though they also pressured the Judahites to participate in the state cult of Marduk. The question is whether the priestly history looks like a program that could be sponsored by the Babylonian rulers, who figured on the restoration of the house of David, or by the Persian government, who at first condoned the house of David but after the rebuilding of the temple did not. Because P treats the priestly shrine as a tent (see chapter 9), we favor the period 538–520 B.C.E.; see also Ernst Axel Knauf, *Ismael: Untersuchungen zur Geschichte Palästinas und Nordarabiens im 1. Jahrtausend v. Chr.*, 2nd ed. (Wiesbaden: Otto Harrassowitz, 1989), 61.

2. The language of P reveals monarchic period features, and it is possible that the Deuteronomistic history and Jeremiah allude to or quote P in the sense of this monarchic period tradition. This is in line with the fact that the traditions are the traditions of the monarchic priesthood. In their present form, however, they are composed in relation to JE, as a result of the restoration of the Zadokite priests, which gave them control of the royal document JE. P was thus confirmed as the primary scriptural authority of the temple by, for example, Ezra, and had its main stipulation, the Sabbath, enforced by Nehemiah, all in the name of Persian imperial sovereignty.

3. A growing number of historians take the view that P is a revision of JE. See Frederick H. Cryer, "The Interrelationships of Gen 5, 32; 11, 10–11 and the Chronology of the Flood (Gen 6–9)," *Biblica* 66 (1985): 244–48; Frank Moore Cross, *Canaanite Myth and Hebrew Epic: Essays in the History of the Religion of Israel* (Cambridge: Harvard University Press, 1973), pp. 293–325 ("The Priestly Work"). A recent critique of this view was argued by Klaus Koch, "P—Kein Redaktor," *Vetus Testamentum* 37 (1987): 446–67. Note also the comments by J. A. Emerton, "The Priestly Writer in Genesis," *Journal of Theological Studies* 39 (1988): 381–400. It may be assumed that most of the traditions and basic conceptions stem from the monarchic period. Many scholars find evidence that the traditions of the priestly strand go back at least to the time of Hezekiah in the late eighth century B.C.E. See M. Haran, "Behind the Scenes of History: Determining the Date of the Priestly Source," *Journal of Biblical Literature* 100 (1981) 321–33; Ziony Zevit, "Converging Lines of Evidence Bearing on the Date of P," *Zeitschrift für die alttestamentliche Wissenschaft* 94 (1982): 481–511; Richard E. Friedman, *Who Wrote the Bible?* (New York: Summit Books, 1987), 171, 207–14. One significant exception to this view is the sevenfold scheme based on the Sabbath as a seven-day period: see chapter 8.

the priestly writer, since Egypt was one of the prime threats to Persian authority in Palestine, and since the Aaronids wanted to pose as loyal to Persia. By siding against Egypt, the priestly writer was discrediting the pro-Egyptian faction in Israel and saying that the pro-Persian party was the one to be loyal to.

In the official history, the brief law promulgated at Sinai was chiefly cult law.[4] The priestly writer could use this slot in the history, beginning in Exodus 25, to insert his main subject, a grand elaboration of the laws of the official Judahite cult.

HISTORICAL SCHEME

The history the priestly writer inherited was structured by sets of seven generations. This resulted in a scheme of three sets of seven generations plus one, for a total of twenty-two generations from creation to the moment when Israel was poised on the brink of the promised land. By implication, the last generation would inherit the promise. The priestly writer modified this generational structure of history so that the first two sets of generations each had ten generations. The third set had seven generations, the seventh being the generation who took possession of the land Israel was to rule. This revised scheme features a total of twenty-seven generations.

In the original history, the great heroes Noah and Abram came at the beginning of their respective sets of seven generations. The priestly writer's arrangement placed these figures at the end of their sets of ten generations. Throughout the priestly work there is a sense of conclusion, finality, completeness, and wholeness, in contrast to the earlier history's sense of open-endedness and inconclusiveness. To preview the climactic nature of the number seven in the generational scheme, in line with the climactic nature of the seventh day of creation, the man of the seventh generation, Enoch, is given the distinction of having "walked with God, and he took him."

The columns in Fig. 1 show that the priestly writer accomplished his structural redesign by adding five new names (in boldface), two at the beginning of his first set of ten generations, and three near the end of his second set of ten generations.[5]

---

4. In J, it was all cult law; E added further laws dealing with other subjects, and these were further expanded, probably under Hezekiah. See Robert B. Coote, *In Defense of Revolution: The Elohist History* (Minneapolis: Fortress, 1991), 117–38.
5. The early part of the JE list can be found in Genesis 4 and 10, while the early part of the P list is found in Genesis 5 and 11. In the first set the JE and P names are not always identical, but they are similar enough to show they are equivalent.

Fig. 1

Royal (JE) and Priestly (P) Generations from Adam to Caleb

JE		P	
1	Adam	1	Adam
2	Cain	2	Seth
3	Enok	3	Enosh
4	Irad	4	Cenan (= Cain)
5	Mehuyael	5	Mahalalel (= Mehuyael)
6	Methushael	6	Yared (= Irad)
7	Lemek	7	Enok
		8	Methushelah (= Methushael)
		9	Lemek
8	Noah	10	Noah
9	Shem	11	Shem
10	Arpahshad	12	Arpachshad
11	Shelah	13	Shelah
12	Eber	14	Eber
13	Peleg	15	Peleg
		16	Re'u
		17	Serug
		18	Nahor
14	Terah	19	Terah
15	Abram	20	Abraham
16	Isaac	21	Isaac
17	Jacob	22	Jacob
18	Levi	23	Levi
19	[ ]	24	Qehat
20	[ ]	25	Amram
21	Moses	26	Moses
22	Caleb	27	Caleb

Why did the priestly writer change the original history's structure? Because he was interested in the numbers 10, 7, and 3. Ten was an especially significant number for the priestly writer. It is the basis of the Hebrew numbering system, like ours, and probably originated from the convenience of counting on ten fingers. It is also the sum of the other two significant numbers in the priestly revision of the cult's history, 7 and 3. Many of the furnishings of the tabernacle and temple, of such importance to the priestly writer, were arranged in

terms of 10.[6] According to one recent historian, the dimensions of
the priestly tabernacle were approximately 10 × 20 × 7 cubits.[7]

The priestly writer's other major modification of the original generational scheme of the history was to introduce a sequence of covenants. There are three covenants, connected with Noah, Abraham,
and Moses—the tenth, twentieth, and twenty-sixth generations. They
are called "eternal" covenants to signify their extreme importance.
Each of these covenants is marked by a special sign and by the use
of a particular term when speaking of or to God:

COVENANT	SIGN	NAME
Covenant of Noah (Gen. 9)	Bow	God
Covenant of Abraham (Gen. 17)	Circumcision	El Shadday
Covenant of Moses (Exod. 6)	Sabbath	Yahweh

Having modified the basic structure of the temple history of the
world, the priestly writer introduced alterations into the narrative
itself in order to express the interests of the Aaronid priesthood. Moses
was the hero of Yahweh's rescue of Israel from Egypt, the climax of
the original history. However, Moses was the hero of the Levite group.
It was therefore advisable for the Aaronid writer to introduce Aaron
as a significant hero. Whereas the original history typically read,
"Yahweh said to Moses . . . ," the priestly writer in many instances
added, "and Aaron." In the earlier history, Moses had a special staff.
In the priestly revision, the staff belongs to Aaron. The earlier history
called Aaron Moses' "Levite brother." The priestly revision makes
sure it is clear that Aaron was the firstborn, thus Moses' older brother.
In the genealogy of the Levites in the priestly revision of the story of
the exodus, Aaron's family is mentioned but not Moses'.[8]

To confirm that the Aaronids held exclusive priestly prerogatives,
the priestly writer modified another of the earlier history's stories.
The revised narrative is in Numbers 16. Originally this text told about
a revolt against Moses' authority by Dathan and Abiram, sons of
Reuben. The revolt ended when the earth opened up and swallowed
them alive. In the priestly writer's additions, the challenge comes from
a group of Levites, headed by Korah, and it is not against Moses but

6. See, for example, Exod. 26, 1 Kings 6–7, 2 Chron. 4, and Ezek 45.
7. Richard E. Friedman, *Who Wrote the Bible?* (New York: Summit Books, 1987), 176–81.
8. Ibid., 190–91.

against "Moses and Aaron." They demand to know why it is that Aaron has an exclusive hold on priestly tasks. Why cannot anyone else perform them? After all, the plaintiffs charge, "All the congregation are holy, every one of them." Moses is portrayed as supporting Aaron. He proposes that everyone claiming priestly prerogatives burn incense before Yahweh and see what happens. They all do, Aaron and the Levites, and "fire came forth from Yahweh and consumed the two hundred and fifty men offering the incense"—everyone except Aaron.

Another priestly narrative duplicates the earlier story in which Moses drew water from a rock (Exod. 17:2-7). In the priestly duplicate in Numbers 20:2-13, Aaron joins Moses. When Moses strikes the rock and water comes out, Yahweh rebukes Moses, with Aaron. "Because you did not believe in me, to sanctify me in the eyes of the people of Israel, therefore you shall not bring this assembly into the land which I have given them." What was an obedient and good act in the earlier history, the priestly writer turns into a disobedient act for which Moses suffers extremely harsh punishment, with Aaron also suffering for what was basically Moses' sin.[9]

Other priestly modifications reinforce the structuring in multiples of ten and three. The entire history prior to the story of Israel itself is covered by the explication of ten sets of genealogies, designated by the heading, "These are the generations of," or, "This is the document of the generations of." This heading first occurs at the seam between the priestly account of creation in Genesis 1:1–2:3 and the earlier account that it now partly supersedes at Genesis 2:4: "These are the generations of the heavens and the earth when they were created." As is clear from the other uses of this heading in the priestly revision of the history, the notice here refers to what follows in the history as it originally appeared rather than to what precedes in the priestly revision. With this heading the priestly writer makes clear that he regards the whole of the original creation account that follows to be an unfolding of what is presented schematically in his own account of creation.

The other headings of this type in Genesis introduce the "generations of" Adam, Noah, the sons of Noah, Shem, Terah, Ishmael,[10]

---

9. Friedman, *Who Wrote the Bible?* 197–201.
10. P's interest in Ishmael is now laid out in Ernst Axel Knauf, *Ismael,* 56–65, 145–47.

Isaac, Esau, and Jacob (Israel). The final heading, "These are the generations of Jacob"[11] (Gen. 37:2), serves to introduce the whole of the rest of the history of Israel—how they came to Egypt and how they got out safely again.[12]

A further priestly structuring device is the delineation of the trek through the wilderness as progressing through six stations before Sinai and six from Sinai to the end, thus positioning Sinai and all it represents at the center of the trek. The references to these stations follow a formula that can be illustrated by the seventh of them, when the assembly of Israel arrive at Sinai. "They journeyed from Rephidim and came to the wilderness of Sinai" (Exod. 19:2). In addition, the priestly writer here gives the date as the third month, probably indicating the priestly view that Israel was at Sinai to receive all the laws of cult and social order from Yahweh at what was to be celebrated as the wheat harvest festival, known as the Feast of Weeks.

PRIESTLY EMPHASES

From the beginning of the history, the priestly writer makes revisions to the narrative itself in order to emphasize priestly points. Unlike the original history, which was nationalist in character, the priestly revisions, under Persian dominion, are cosmic in scope. It is the priestly writer who turns the original story of the first great rain into the universal flood of the present text of Noah. The original history called the rain *geshem,* "downpour"; the priestly revision calls it *mabbul,* "great flood." In the original history, it simply rained; in the priestly revision, "all the fountains of the great deep burst forth and the windows of heaven were opened." In the original history, the rain lasted forty days and nights. The priestly writer notes that the flood came in Noah's six-hundredth year, a multiple of ten and six, and lasted exactly one year and ten days.[13]

In the original history, Noah took on board seven pairs of clean animals and one pair of unclean ones. In the priestly revision, he takes one pair of all animals regardless. Why does the original history make a distinction between clean and unclean animals that might be thought

11. RSV: "This is the history of the family of Jacob."
12. The brief presentation of the generations of Aaron in Num. 3:1–3 falls outside this scheme.
13. P's chronological scheme for the flood is actually a good deal more complicated than this, though equally schematic and arithmetic. See Frederick H. Cryer, "The Interrelationships of Gen. 5, 32; 11, 10-11 and the Chronology of the Flood (Gen. 6–9)," *Biblica* 66 (1985): 244–48.

more appropriate to a priestly writer, whose concern was with animals fit for sacrifice? Have historians assigned authorship of this passage to J when it should have been assigned to P? Not at all. In the original history, Noah required extra animals for the sacrifice he would make after the downpour. In the priestly revision there is no sacrifice, since there is not yet a consecrated priesthood. That does not come until Sinai. There is not even a definition of what constitutes a clean animal; this comes only when the specifications of the third eternal covenant are given at Sinai.

The priestly writer has a particular understanding of the flood that does not exist in the original history. He is disturbed that blood is being poured out on the earth without a priest present to supervise the procedure, as occurs when Cain kills Abel, near the beginning of the whole story. The violence continues with Lemek's killing a man (Gen. 4:23). By the time of the generation of Noah, the priestly writer sees the earth as filled with violence and corruption (Gen. 6:11-13). It has become polluted, and God must send a flood to wash away the pollution from the world. "The flood is not primarily an agency of punishment . . . but a means of getting rid of a thoroughly polluted world and starting again with a clean, well-washed one."[14] In the priestly view, the flood represents a cosmic cleansing.

The cosmic scope of the priestly writer can also be seen in his modifications of the Exodus narrative of the plagues of Egypt. He adds to the stories of individual plagues. For example, according to the original history, the plague of blood affected only the Nile River. But the priestly writer adds, "Yahweh said to Moses, 'Say to Aaron, "Take your rod and stretch out your hand over the waters of Egypt, over their rivers, their canals, and their ponds, and all their pools of water, that they may become blood; and there shall be blood through-out all the land of Egypt." ' " The term translated "pools of water" is the rare term translated "the waters that were gathered together" in Genesis 1:10. "Its use in Exod. 7:19 could not fail to evoke an association with Gen. 1:10 and an intimation of the cosmic import of the plague."[15] The priestly writer modified the plague of frogs in a similar way. "P's decision to describe the plague [of frogs] as one

14. Tikva Frymer-Kensky, "The Atrahasis Epic and its Significance for our Understanding of Genesis 1–9," *Biblical Archaeologist* 40 (1977): 153.
15. Ziony Zevit, "The Priestly Redaction and Interpretation of the Plague Narrative in Exodus," *Jewish Quarterly Review* 66 (1976): 193–211, especially p. 199.

which involved all of Egypt may be explained in terms of his familiarity with Gen. 1. The verb *sharats,* 'swarm,' in JE, Exod. 7:28, was associated with Gen. 1:20, 'Let the waters *swarm* with *swarms* of living creatures . . . ' and Gen. 1:22, 'God blessed them saying: Be fruitful and multiply, fill the waters in the seas.' "[16]

The priestly revision adds two plagues to the original history's eight, to bring the total up to ten. One of the added plagues is lice.

> By the insertion of the lice plague into the narrative in between the frog and fly plagues, P created a pattern in which creatures associated respectively with water, land, and heavens so filled the land of Egypt that they interrupted the normal affairs of the Egyptians. This situation was a complete reversal of the one anticipated by the divine blessing to mankind in Gen. 1:28: "Be fruitful, multiply, fill the earth, master it. Rule the fish of the sea, the winged creatures of the heavens, and all living creatures which creep on the earth."[17]

The other plague added by the priestly writer is boils, in line with his interest in skin diseases in Leviticus 13. "P's image of Egypt at the conclusion of his plague-exodus narratives is of a land with no people, no animals, no vegetation—a land in which creation was undone,"[18] in allusion to Genesis 1.

This then is the distinctive character of the priestly version of the Jerusalem temple's history of the world, preserved by Zadokite Aaronid hands at the beginning of the Persian period in Babylon and Palestine. The extant JE narrative has been structurally rationalized so as to become a more suitable literary vehicle for the recording and transmission of the basic cultic rules and taboos of the Aaronids and the customary laws of the temple jurisdiction over which they presided during the Davidic monarchy and Persian period.

16. Ibid., 202.
17. Ibid., 205.
18. Ibid., 210.

5

Everything Falls
into Place

The priestly creation story in Genesis 1:1—2:4a comes first in the
Bible for no other reason than that it introduces the Aaronid revision
of the Davidic monarchic temple history. This revision sets forth how
the Aaronid priests of the late sixth-century B.C.E. viewed the world
they lived in and how they imagined that world had come into being.
The Aaronids remained the dominant priesthood of the replacement
temple throughout its existence, and hence their revision became the
established version of the authoritative scriptural history.

Thus Genesis 1 is not a general, universal account of creation. It
is an account specifically derived from and relating to the cult of the
late sixth-century Aaronids in Persian Babylon and Jerusalem. Like
nearly all the accounts of creation known from the ancient Near East,
it is part of a tradition whose primary concern is a sacrificial state
cult. Such traditions were often recorded when the cult was refounded
and hence required reconceptualization and a reconfirmation of priestly theory.

But although Genesis 1 is the product of a priesthood of a religious
cult, like these other creation stories, the view of creation in Genesis
1 is related to the social situation from which it springs. The creation
of the world is directly linked to such realities as food, population,
and land tenure. It is the account of how there came into being the
world of the late sixth-century B.C.E. Jerusalemite priesthood, a land-
holding elite in their local context, clients to the Persian imperial court
in the wider context, whose primary function was to conduct an
animal sacrificial rite ostensibly on behalf of the townspeople and
villagers of the Persian province of Palestine.

There is a broad sense of integration and comprehensiveness in the priestly view as laid out here. Everything of importance is interrelated. The categories and structures established in Genesis 1 constitute the spring from which everything in the priestly reconstruction of history flows, the seed from which all grows, the bud from which all blossoms.

WHEN GOD BEGAN . . .

It was typical of ancient Near Eastern creation accounts to begin with a parenthetical statement describing the circumstances that were present at the time of creation. Thus the Babylonian creation account *Enuma elish* begins:

> When on high the heaven had not been named, firm ground below had not been called by name, naught but primordial Apsu, their begetter, and Tiamat, she who bore them all, their waters comingling as a single body; no reed hut had been matted, no marsh land had appeared, when no gods whatever had been brought into being, uncalled by name, their destinies undetermined—

All this is said before the first "event" of creation actually occurs:

> Then it was that the gods were formed within them.[1]

Genesis 1 is a typical creation account, so it opens the same way. The traditional translation says, "In the beginning God created the heavens and the earth." This (thus also the title of this book) is incorrect. Historians are generally aware of this, but translations continue to render the Hebrew in this way because it is so traditional. Genesis 1 actually begins like the *Enuma elish,* with a parenthetical statement telling what it was like prior to the first act of creation, which itself was when God ordered light to exist:

> The first thing God did when he created the sky and earth—at that time, the earth had no form or structure, darkness was over the surface of the ocean, and the wind of God was hovering just above the surface of the water—was to say, "Let light come into existence." So light came into existence.

Readers of the creation story of Genesis 1 are frequently puzzled by the statement that the first thing God created was "sky and earth."

1. *ANET,* pp. 60–61, lines 1–9.

They observe that although the text says God created sky and earth on the first day, it was not until the second day, when God made the "firmament," that the sky came into being. They also note that although light and darkness, day and night, are said to have been created on this same first day, it is not until the fourth day that the sun, moon, and stars were made. The answer to this puzzle is that the opening statement that God created "sky and earth" is a summary anticipating the whole of what follows. It refers not to individual parts of the created order, but to the complete structure and organization described for the full six days of creation. In similar manner the narrator summarizes in 2:1: "Thus the heavens and the earth were finished, and all the host of them."

Obviously much did already exist, however, at the first moment of creation. The ocean was present. The word for ocean is related to the Babylonian word for Tiamat. The RSV follows the traditional rendering "deep," which perhaps was meant to suggest an abyss of nothing, whereas it actually should suggest deep water. A wind likewise existed. As creation begins, the scene involves an ocean, in the darkness, with the wind blowing. Something already exists, but what is not present is order. Nothing distinctive of human life and of importance to social existence in sixth-century B.C.E. Palestine under the surrogate rule of land-holding priests is present.

ORDER IN SIX DAYS

The world prior to creation is a disordered world. It is not so much void as unorganized. The substantive points made by the creation account are not just that God created this and that, but that he did so in a particular order in time and for a particular order in space.[2]

Yet God does not so much *make* things out of disorder as summon or *command* them out of disorder. The first act of creation is a statement: "Let light be." This is not an invitation but a command, an order. Creation in the priestly history consists mainly of a series of commands. Throughout the priestly history God gives commands, and people are obedient to those commands, much the way an Aaronid might have issued commands in the temple organization and expected

2. There is now quite clear evidence from the Ugaritic texts that the partly mysterious Hebrew *tohu wabohu* in Gen. 1:2 (RSV: "without form and void") meant "out of order, unproductive." See David Toshio Tsumura, *"Nabalkutu, tu-a-bi-[u]* and *tohu wabohu,"* *Ugarit-Forschungen* 19 (1987): 309–15.

to be immediately obeyed. The created order is no different. The whole cosmos is obedient. When the principle of obedience is violated, as when someone commits a sin, some component of the created order will have to operate to resolve that violation. This is the basic purpose of the sacrificial rite of the tabernacle that is central to the Aaronid priestly writer.

Darkness already exists. The first thing God creates is light. The alternation between darkness and light marks the unit of time called the day. This is the unit of time that the priestly writer selects to organize his account of creation.[3] The six days of creation, followed by a seventh day of rest, will play a significant role at the climax of the priestly reconstruction of history. It is appropriate therefore for God to create this unit first. Because darkness preceded light in the created order, the ancient Israelites thought of the day as beginning at sundown rather than midnight or dawn. This idea was widespread long before the priestly tradition came into being, and the priestly account may be an accommodation to it.

Next we are told that "God separated the light from the darkness." Separating, making a distinction, categorizing—these are of the essence of the creative process in the priestly conception. God proceeds to organize the world through this process of separating and categorizing over a period of six days:

DAYS 1, 2, 3	DAYS 4, 5, 6
Light	Sun, moon, stars
Firmament	Animals in the sea, fish, birds
Land, plants	Animals, humans

At first glance this order of creation may appear arbitrary, especially when seen through the prose narrative in which it is presented. The plan of creation follows a clear pattern, however, as can be seen when the terms of the above chart are described slightly differently:

3. A glance back at chapters 1 and 2 will show that such a plan is by no means inevitable in an account of creation.

DAYS 1, 2, 3	DAYS 4, 5, 6
Light	**Moving** *lights*
Firmament, which separates the *waters* above from those below	**Moving** beings in the *waters* above and below
Land, from which spring plants, which do not move	**Moving** beings on *land:* first animals, then humans

Days 1, 2, and 3 define light, water, and land. These may be regarded as the basic elements of creation. They cover sky and earth and the light by which these appear.

Note that both sea and sky consist of water in the ancient view. The *raqia‘,* or "firmament," is a hard translucent dome that divides the waters of the universe in two. The water above the dome is called sky, below the dome sea. We can see the water above any day when it is not obscured by clouds. The blue beyond, in the ancient view, is an extension of the same element seen in the blue sea below. Later, in the time of the great flood, God will open the "windows of heaven" to allow the waters above the dome to pour down upon the earth.

Land comes into being when the water below is reorganized so as to allow land to appear, as though land also already existed and only required a certain order to prevail for it to come into view. From the land, plants emerge and stay in place.

Everything created in the first three days, in the first column, is fixed in place. Everything created in the second three days, in the second column, follows the order of the light, water, and land established in the first three days, but it moves.

LIFE, MOTION, BLOOD

How are the entities of the second three days to be designated or categorized? Are they animate? Alive? Able to move? Denizens of the realms established in the first three days? They are all of these. Even the lights in the sky—the sun, moon, and stars—fall into the category of animate beings, in line with the ancient conception that the heavenly bodies were gods. In addition they are assigned rule, the sun and moon over day and night, the humans over the sea and land animals. But the basic idea is that they move.

The priestly author is particularly interested in the character of moving things, since his main prerogative, eating meat and serving meat to God, requires him to stop animals moving by killing them.

The movement of these created entities raises the question of what makes it possible to keep moving. They are alive, but what keeps them alive? To stay alive, a creature has to eat, and it has to hold on to its blood. These two concerns will be central to the priestly history as it develops. The underlying element of the rites of the priesthood is the disposition of blood. The sequence runs from meat to butchering to a theoretical interest in blood, so that all the basic taboos prescribed in the priestly tradition, particularly in the book of Leviticus, stem from this concern with blood.

Just as the primary feature of the created entities of the second three days is their movement, so when God is finished creating the realms of life and the living things that move in those realms, God stops moving, in a Sabbath rest.

Another difference between the first and second columns above is in reproduction. In the priestly conception, the creatures in the second column reproduce by heterosexual means, while plants in contrast clone themselves. Thus the writer explains that "the earth brought forth vegetation, plants yielding seed according to their own kinds, and trees bearing fruit in which is their seed, each according to its kind." Like plants, moving things also reproduce "according to their kinds"—that is, repeating the same characteristics from generation to generation—except that they reproduce in pairs. God created the creatures in the water "according to their kinds," every bird "according to its kind," the wild animals "according to their kinds," the domestic beasts "according to their kinds," and all the insects "according to their kinds." All these living things were to reproduce their kinds, and to this end God gave them orders to "be fruitful and many and fill the earth." The projected abundance of living things was the basis of the social prosperity that the priests presumed to foster and of which they were primary beneficiaries.

Of what "kind" were the humans? They were not said to be of their own kind. Instead, as God commented to a lesser god in his presence, "Let us make humans in our image, after our likeness. . . . So God created humans in his own image; in the image of God he created them." When they reproduced, this was the image that they passed on: "When God created humans, he made them in the likeness

of God. . . . When Adam had lived a hundred and thirty years, he
became the father of a son in his own likeness, after his image" (Gen.
5:1, 3).

This view of the exalted character of humans is the distinctively
priestly view seen already in the statement in Psalm 8 that God had
"made humans little less than God." It understands humans to be
modeled after the ideal of the divine. In the appearance of the ideal
human being something godlike can be perceived. Hence it is appropriate, in this priestly view, to categorize humans according to the
closeness with which they fulfill this ideal. God does not have faulty
or missing body parts, or detestable skin diseases, or oozing sores,
so humans who suffer these, since they are less like God than those
who do not, must be lesser humans. Such humans are not fit to serve
in the priesthood of the tabernacle or temple.

The broadest command to multiply and rule is given to humans,
and by implication to the elite among humans, especially the ruling
priesthood, who did in fact obey the order more completely than
others. In the narrative and genealogical construction of the priestly
history, considerable stress is placed on the fulfillment of this command
by Israel in general.[4]

Like the other animals, humans were to be male and female and
to be "fruitful" heterosexually rather than by cloning. This order of
creation was inviolable like the rest; hence the strictures against ho-
mosexual behavior in Leviticus 20.

Finally, God makes provision for the moving beings to continue
moving:

> God said, "Behold, I have given you every plant yielding seed
> which is upon the face of all the earth, and every tree with seed in
> its fruit; you shall have them for food. And to every beast of the
> earth, and to every bird of the air, and to everything that creeps
> on the earth, everything that has the breath of life, I have given
> every green plant for food."

All the entities in the second column are assigned plants for food. In
the world order established up to this point, they are not to eat one

---

4. Walter Brueggemann, in "The Kerygma of the Priestly Writers," takes this to be the main
theme of the entire priestly strand, as though it were P's most central point. It would indeed
have been essential in the view of the post-exilic Aaronids. See further Jeremy Cohen, *"Be Fertile
and Increase, Fill the Earth and Master It": The Ancient and Medieval Career of a Biblical Text* (Ithaca:
Cornell University Press, 1989).

another, in order not to shed blood, which as the primary priestly
prerogative must be carefully controlled and find its orderly place in
the created cosmos.

This instruction is violated in the shedding of blood by Cain and
Lemek, and the continued bloody violence (RSV: "corruption") that
in the priestly writer's view makes the flood necessary. Immediately
after the flood, when the earth has been washed clean of this disorderly
shedding of blood, the order for shedding blood is commanded to
Noah. This concern, basic to the question of what meat is proper to
eat in God's created order, is introduced in the account of creation in
Genesis 1.

After each day of creation, God views what has been created and
makes a judgment about whether it is good or bad. As it turns out,
God pronounces everything good. All the parts are in order; everything has its proper place and function.

From this perspective, change is regarded as a departure from the
order established by God in the beginning, with the exception of those
few things changed by God himself through the eternal covenants (in
which animals are assigned for food in addition to plants, and some
skin is removed from the male's penis as originally created). In the
priestly view, the world as it was created was good. Change is bad.
The world established with the Aaronid priesthood at its center is
good. Anything else is bad.

When it is all over, God rests. This Sabbath rest becomes the sign
of the last and most complete—and most exclusive—of the priestly
covenants.

The structure of what follows in the priestly history is prefigured
in the number of times the priestly writer reports that God said, saw,
and blessed. God "said" ten times, God "saw" seven times, and God
"blessed" three times.[5] Thus the priestly writer lays down at the outset
the pattern of occurrence that serves in the sequel as the basis of time
and space in God's created order.

---

5. The traditional Hebrew text preserves the original pattern, conforming to the sacred numbers.
The Greek translation adds "and God saw" at 1:8b, spoiling the pattern.

6

Living in the Lap of Luxury

It is ironic that to understand Genesis 1, a well-known text, it is necessary to refer to many texts that are not so well known, texts having to do with the privileges of priests.

DISTINCTIONS

A main function of the priesthood was, as Leviticus 10:10 expresses it, to "distinguish between the holy and the common, and between the clean and the unclean." The centrality of this function could hardly be overstated. "Distinguish" is exactly what God did in the first act of creation: in Hebrew, God "distinguished" light and darkness. The priestly tradition understood this distinguishing, this separating, to be integral to the inceptive divine act, and the priesthood fell in line with this act, functioning as a distinguished class. Distinctions were the basis of priestly privilege.

In the priestly view, it was necessary not only to make distinctions, but to make them sharply. The model for sharp distinctions was the first: every distinction in the created order should embody a difference like the difference between night and day (Gen. 1:4, 14, 18), or like the cosmic barrier (the "firmament") that made a sharp separation between the sky waters above and sea waters below (Gen. 1:6, 7).

EATING MEAT

The priests' job was to define the distinction between the holy and common, and between the clean and unclean. What was uncommon, or scarce, was declared holy. What the priests who composed Genesis

1 regarded as most uncommon was meat. Meat was not a common
part of the daily diet in the ancient Eastern Mediterranean world.[1]
The staples of the diet in Palestine were bread and olives. There were
other foods in the diet, but these two were far and away the main
ones. To eat meat day in and day out was an extraordinary privilege
in an ancient agrarian society. The priests used their right to delineate
what was holy or common to control the nation's meat supply and
to "rule over" and give themselves access to meat in large quantities.
Much of what was brought to the altar for sacrifice, they ate. From
the priestly perspective, to eat meat was the essence of the holy in
contrast to the common.

In the priestly view, meat as food was not part of the original order
of creation. Creatures were to eat plants, not other creatures. But
after God had washed the earth, which had been "corrupted" with
bloodshed, in the flood, he established a covenant with Noah, all
humanity, and "every living creature that is with you, the birds, the
cattle, and every beast of the earth with you . . . every living creature
of all flesh that is upon the earth" (Gen. 9:10, 16-17). This is the first
of three eternal covenants in the priestly strand. This covenant was
not just with Noah or the people, but with all flesh, because it had
mainly to do with eating "flesh," or meat.

The covenant of Noah bestowed order upon bloodshed, which had
become rampant and, according to the priestly tradition, was the main
reason God sent the flood. The blood shed in murder provided the
occasion for addressing the more common issue of blood shed in the
taking of flesh for food:

> God blessed Noah and his sons, and said to them, "Be fruitful and
> multiply, and fill the earth. The fear of you and the dread of you
> shall be upon every beast of the earth, and upon every bird of the
> air, upon everything that creeps on the ground and all the fish of
> the sea; into your hand they are delivered. Every moving thing
> that lives shall be food for you; and as I gave you the green plants,
> I hereby give you everything. Only you shall not eat flesh with its
> life, that is, its blood. For your lifeblood I shall require a reckoning;
> of every beast I shall require it, and of humans; of every human's
> kin I shall require the life of a human. Whoever sheds the blood of

---

1. See Fernand Braudel, *The Mediterranean and the Mediterranean World in the Age of Philip II*, vol.
1 (New York: Harper & Row, 1972), 239–46, 459.

a human, by a human shall their blood be shed;[2] for God made humans in his own image. Be fruitful and multiply, bring forth abundantly on the earth and multiply in it."

Blood was the element of life in the body in the priestly view. "For the life of every creature is the blood of it; therefore I have said to the people of Israel, You shall not eat the blood of any creature, for the life of every creature is its blood; whoever eats it shall be cut off" (Lev. 17:14). The eating of blood was forbidden by repeated injunctions (Lev. 3:17; 7:26, 27; 17:10–16; and 19:26).

Each covenant has a sign. The sign of the covenant sanctioning the orderly shedding of blood, which made possible the eating of meat for the first time, is the bow. In Hebrew as in English, the word "bow" signifies both a bow for shooting arrows and the rainbow. However, the Hebrews did not think of these as unrelated, as we do today. To them, they were one and the same. What God placed in the clouds as a "sign of the covenant which I have established between me and all flesh" was a bow. The bow was the first, primitive instrument with which humans would shed the blood of an animal they intended to eat, and hence it was an appropriate sign of the covenant of meat eating. The covenant includes God's promise never again to wash away "all flesh," who were shedding blood indiscriminately and polluting the ground, by opening up the windows of the sky to let the cosmic waters flood onto the earth. The bow ratifies this promise by signifying the arc of the firmament, which spans from horizon to horizon and holds back the cosmic waters above it.

WHAT MEAT?

When God sanctions the eating of meat at the time of the first covenant, all flesh is assigned as food. But when the third covenant, the covenant of Moses, is inaugurated, not all creatures are henceforth to be considered edible. As Leviticus 11:47 expresses it, in addition to determining what was holy or common, it was a priestly function "to make a distinction between the unclean and the clean, namely between the living creature that may be eaten and the living creature that may not be eaten." How the priests classified animals as clean or unclean, edible or taboo, depended on how closely a creature matched the

---

2. This is a limiting clause: no person, no matter how powerful, may murder indiscriminately as Cain and Lemek had done and expect to escape God's retribution.

order established during the seven days of creation and the three
priestly covenants. The meat of some creatures was edible because
they were closer to the original order of creation than other creatures.

The centrality of the process of distinguishing—first between the
holy and the common, then between the clean and the unclean—was
rooted in the separating activity of God in the creation story, extended
in the first covenant, and delineated explicitly in the third covenant.
To appreciate how this theme undergirds the whole of the priestly
tradition, it is necessary to notice where in the organization of the
priestly history the necessary distinctions in meat are defined. A brief
scheme of the whole of the priestly history makes this clear:

1. Creation
2. Covenant of Noah (bow)
3. Covenant of Abraham (circumcision)
4. Covenant of Moses (Sabbath)
   a. Tabernacle, altar, and priests
   b. The sacrifices, followed by ordination of the priests
   c. Taboos regarding blood and spotting
   d. Laws for maintaining the holiness of the people, begin-
      ning with controls on the disposition of blood
   e. Other laws

In this scheme, the definition of clean and unclean flesh, which is
presented in Leviticus 11, comes at the beginning of the section concerning taboos regarding blood (4c). This section comprises Leviticus
11–16. The laws in this section deal with flesh allowed for eating;
circumcision, along with the purification of a woman after childbirth;
spotted diseases of skin, clothing, and walls; discharges of blood, pus,
semen; and a ritual of general composition, which the RSV refers to
by the term "atonement." (Composition is a legal term having to do
with the settling, or composing, of differences. An imbalance that
results from damage or a deprivation has to be made right. Equilibrium
is restored by the transfer of something of value. The concept of
composition is the same as the concept of *shalom*, in which a state of
justice and well-being prevails.) This will be discussed further in
chapter 10.

All these laws are found in the same section of the priestly history
because they involve the killing of animals, either directly for food
(Leviticus 11) or in ritual settlement (composition) for all necessary

situations not covered by the sacrifices prescribed in Leviticus 1–7 (Leviticus 12–16). Such situations may seem varied to the modern reader, but they all have one thing in common: they involve the discharging, oozing, or spotting of blood, bloodlike body fluids, or, in the case of the spotted diseases, bloodlike blotches, especially as concerns the reproductive functions by which humans fulfill the creation command to be "fruitful" (fruits do not bleed) and multiply. They are a function not only of the priestly obsession with the disposition of blood, but also of the appearance (the diseases appear as surface phenomena, even though they may actually go deeper) of blood in the daily rites of the priests.

The priests often took an ideal approach to their own purity. Among the class of priests who are of particular interest in this book, no one who could not meet rigorous standards could serve as a priest:

> Yahweh said to Moses, "Say to Aaron that none of your descendants throughout their generations who has a defect may approach to offer up the food of his God. For no one who has any of the following defects may come forward: he who is blind, or lame, or who has any disfigurement or malformation, or a crippled foot or hand, or who is humpbacked, dwarfish, or walleyed, or who is afflicted with eczema, ringworm, or hernia. No descendant of Aaron the priest who has any such defect may draw near to offer up the oblations of Yahweh; on account of his defect he may not draw near to offer up the food of his God." (Lev. 21:16-21, based on NAB)

In the conception of these idealists, animals for sacrifice to God had to meet the same requirements of purity:

> If it is to be acceptable, the ox or sheep or goat that he offers must be an unblemished male. You shall not offer one that has any defect, for such a one would not be acceptable for you. . . . It must be unblemished; it shall not have any defect. One that is blind or crippled or maimed, or one that has a running sore or mange or ringworm, you shall not offer to Yahweh. . . . An ox or a sheep that is in any way ill-proportioned or stunted you may indeed present as a voluntary offering, but it will not be acceptable as a votive offering. One that has its testicles bruised or crushed or torn out or cut off you shall not offer to Yahweh. . . . Since they are deformed or defective, they will not be acceptable for you (Lev. 21:19-25, based on NAB).

LEVITICUS 11

The priestly preoccupation with order extends to the "purity" of the animals eaten. This purity is defined by the distinction between one kind of flesh and another. This distinction, described in Leviticus 11, holds first position in the section of the priestly tradition that immediately follows the basic institutions of tabernacle, priesthood, and sacrifice, and elaborates on the disposition of blood. The distinctions are the main subject of the priestly tradition after the primary issue of the peculiar sacrificial ritual functions of the priesthood, which center on the shedding of animal blood to prepare flesh for food for God, the priests, and some of the people.

The translation of a number of the terms for different species mentioned in the rules for eating meat in Leviticus 11 is not always clear, but the text is clear enough to understand the set of rules perfectly well.

The priestly writers were highly conscious of the categories of animals and how distinct they were from one another, as a scientist might be conscious of the distinctiveness of different species. This is shown in Leviticus 19:19, which warns against the mixing of different types of animals, as well as plants:

> You shall not let your cattle breed with a different kind. You shall not sow your field with two kinds of seed; nor shall there come upon you a garment of cloth made of two kinds of stuff.

The categories of animals follow the categories of creation, though not the order: land, water below, sky. Hence the prescription deals with animals according to the following categories: land animals; fish and other sea animals; birds, then flying insects and hopping insects.

The principles for discerning whether a creature of the land is clean are spelled out first:

> Land animals that have a hoof, are cloven-hooved, and chew the cud.

The principle for discerning which sea creatures are clean is spelled out next: "Sea animals that have fins and scales."

The principles governing the cleanness of the third category of creatures, those of the sky, are not stated expressly but can be deduced from the birds specified as unclean. Sky creatures that do not eat meat or walk on land or water are clean, as are insects with wings that walk on land and have legs for hopping.

The conditions a creature must meet before it can be considered fit for food are tied to the characteristics that define what is normative for a creature in a particular realm, whether it be a creature of the land, water, or sky. For the priests who composed this tradition there was an original created order, and things were clean when they abode by that order. There was an ideal type of animal suited for the land, an ideal for the water, and an ideal for the sky. The principle the priestly writer lays down is that each type of creature was intended to be tied to a single realm. When a creature deviates from the realm for which it was originally created, it violates the ideal and is unclean.

The fundamental issue in determining cleanness is whether a creature is in some way "blemished" with regard to the realm for which it was created according to the priestly ordering of the world in Genesis 1. Those creatures that fit into more than one realm, or do not conform to the model for a particular realm, are blemished. That is, they show traits of being disorderly. Uncleanness, in other words, is a matter of disorder; it is becoming mixed in with a realm to which the creature does not belong.

The primary requirement for cleanness has to do with the creature's mode of locomotion. This interest in the way creatures move is based on the observation that those parts of creation that came into being on days four, five, and six of the creation week (column two in the chart on page 53), and were intended to populate the realms of land, sea, and sky that had been created on days one, two, and three (column one in the chart), all move. But there is a proper way to move within a realm. An animal's means of locomotion should be suited to the realm it lives in: hoofs for land, fins for water, wings for sky.

The mode of locomotion is not, however, of itself sufficient to define what is normative for a creature of a particular realm, so the priestly writer added a second requirement. For the realms of land and sky, this second requirement is diet—whether the creature is an eater of plants or an eater of other creatures. A creature that eats plants and not other creatures is closer to the original order of creation and therefore potentially clean. For the realm of the waters, where presumably the priests could not necessarily discern what creatures ate, the second requirement has to do with the creature's outer covering.

Although the rules are presented as though derived from the order established at creation, in actuality this order was itself derived from the habits of sacrifice and eating that were prevalent in Palestine. The land animals basic to the lives and economy of Palestinians were oxen, sheep, and goats—domesticated livestock. These are cloven-hooved and chew the cud. To have hooves is not to have claws. Claws are for seizing, tearing, and holding prey, and so indicate blood-shedding and blood-eating creatures rather than plant-eating creatures. Chewing the cud is taken as a mark of cleanness because, if it is good to eat plants, it must be even better to eat them several times over. The most common domestic ruminants, cattle and sheep, set the standard for land animals, and the requirement that the hoof be cloven seems to derive from this characteristic of their makeup.

The priestly rationalist was interested in sharply demarcated categories, so he rejected animals that do not fulfill the full quota of criteria. The camel, rock hyrax, and hare chew so thoroughly and often that they appear to chew the cud, but have neither cloven hooves nor true hooves. The pig has a cloven hoof but does not chew the cud. None of these animals is therefore clean.

PRIESTLY RATIONALE

There has been considerable discussion of the reasons for the biblical injunction against eating pork. Much that has been written on the subject deals with pork alone without recognizing the overall pattern of food taboos given in the priestly tradition. The reason is probably a combination of ecological, political, and theoretical factors. All these factors would have applied for the Jerusalemite ruling priesthood of the early Persian period in Palestine, when Persian control and priestly authority were both at their highest level. Where pigs are avoided, antelope tend to be eaten in greater quantity. Antelope do of course fulfill the criteria for cleanness in the priestly scheme.[3]

3. Marvin Harris's explanation that pigs are costly to raise in the Middle East because of the lack of natural feeding places, requiring them to be fed only on food that would otherwise go directly to people, suggests much that may have been true of pig raising in biblical times: *Cows, Pigs, Wars, and Witches: The Riddles of Culture* (New York: Vintage Books, 1978), 28–50. Moreover, pig aversion was not limited to Palestine, just as might be expected in Harris's view. Herodotus reported that pigs were also unclean to Egyptians (2:46f). Yet there were many places in Palestine in biblical times where wild pigs could forage, and domestic pigs have been raised in great numbers despite the disadvantages in many periods in Palestine history. Nevertheless it is clear even from the primary category of clean animals that the norm is set according to existing practice, and some material factor in the raising of pigs probably played a role in the Israelite or priestly

The first characteristic that must be possessed by creatures of the waters if they are to be considered edible is fins. In the waters, fins are the appropriate mode of locomotion. Those that walk or swarm in water, like octopus, crabs, and shrimp, or that snake or fly through the water, like eels or rays, do not qualify. A second characteristic is the outer covering of the creature. This must be scales, rather than skin. Creatures with skin, such as sharks and dolphins, do not qualify because skin is a characteristic of creatures of the land.

As for creatures of the sky, birds that walk on the ground and do not fly, like the ostrich, are disqualified because they violate the appropriate means of locomotion for creatures of the sky. Birds that walk or float in the water, even though they fly, are also unclean, because flying is not their main mode of locomotion. This would apply to the heron and duck, among many others, which are not strictly "birds of the air" but waterfowl. So too birds that eat live or dead meat do not qualify, as they violate the original prescription to eat plants. The model for clean birds is the dove, which eats seeds and flies as its principle means of locomotion. The bat is unclean both because it eats meat and because it does not have feathers and wings like normal creatures of the air.

"Swarming things," which swarm on land and in water and sky, are unclean because they have no clear-cut form of locomotion peculiar to their realm of motion. Flying insects, for example, fly around in the air and then walk around on all fours or sixes. Grasshoppers, locusts, and crickets are an exception: they have wings and they hop, which the priests regarded as a form of flight. This last case was ambiguous enough for those who composed the laws of Deuteronomy to take a different stance: there such insects are unclean with the rest (Deut. 14).

---

avoidance of pigs. Hesse and Wapnish have recently suggested that Harris's ecological approach be modified or supplemented with two political factors that played a role in Palestinian agriculture over the ages. First, pig raising has periodically been a way for small farmers to raise cash and avoid state control through taxation of livestock. Second, as suggested by Coon, when monoculture of the cash crops of olives and grapes occurs, usually under state encouragement or control, the territory and resources available for pig foraging are reduced and pigs are officially shunned. In this view, official pig avoidance is a function not of the high cost of raising pigs, which is not a problem for a ruling or priestly elite, but of a strong central state. The archaeological evidence for Palestine indicates practically no pig use for the periods both of early Israel and monarchic Israel. See Brian Hesse, "Animal Use at Tel Miqne-Ekron in the Bronze Age and Iron Age," *Bulletin of the American Schools of Oriental Research* 264 (1986): 17–27; U. Hübner, "Schweine, Schweineknochen und ein Speiseverbot im alten Israel," *Vetus Testamentum* 39 (1989): 225–36.

Genesis 1 may thus be said to have been generated out of a set of cultural givens rationalized to a relatively high state of system and order. It represents the tradition or composition of an ascendant priesthood. Its categories reflect in an important way the cultural given that the priesthood assumed the custodianship of cultic sacrifice and the privilege of eating meat in quantity, both traced to the function of disposing properly of blood, the element of motion and of life itself. Many of the priestly taboos were part of the life of the people long before they were recorded in the priestly history. But the particularly thorough and systematic organization seen in the priestly writings, and the retrojection of the basis for this order back to the creation of world order as seen in Genesis 1, are the distinctive contribution of the exilic or early Persian Aaronid priesthood of Jerusalem.

7

Women: Keep Out

The sign of God's second covenant, the covenant with Abraham, is circumcision. It is widely thought that the priestly tradition placed great importance on circumcision as a mark of identity in exile. But the notion that the custom became prominent at the supposed beginning of the Jewish Diaspora presents many difficulties.

CIRCUMCISION, IDENTITY, AND LOYALTY

In the first place, few Judahites lived outside Palestine. Even during the Babylonian exile, it was essentially only the Jerusalemite elite who resided beyond the boundaries of their native country. That circumcision was practiced within the borders of the Judahite nation hardly indicates that it was a way of keeping Jews separate from Babylonians.

Also, if circumcision functioned as a sign of identity, it was not exactly conspicuous, considering the Judahites wore clothes in public. Because of its private nature, it could serve as a sign of identity only among those who were already so intimately associated with one another that they would not need such a sign to determine identity. In this respect, circumcision was quite unlike the signs of the other two priestly covenants—the bow and the Sabbath—which were noticeable to everyone. Only the ritual of cutting might have made its practitioners conspicuous—an important qualification.

Moreover, circumcision could scarcely be the basis of ethnic distinctiveness, since it was a widespread practice. It certainly did not distinguish the Judahite from his neighbor to the south. Egyptians practiced circumcision at least a thousand years before Israelites did and fifteen hundred years before the writing down of Aaronid priestly traditions in the form in which we have them in the priestly revision of the temple scrolls. There is even a report of a male figurine from Palestine showing circumcision going back to the time of the Early Bronze Age in the third millennium B.C.E. Further, Jeremiah, a near contemporary of the priestly writer, identifies the Egyptians, Edomites, Ammonites, Moabites, and Arabs as neighboring peoples who practiced circumcision (Jer. 9:25-26). The practice was in fact extremely common at different times in history, and among neighbors of the Judahites the only notable exception may have been the Philistines, who for several centuries were designated with the epithet "uncircumcised."

Most troublesome for the view that circumcision was an identifying mark is that Abraham is described by the priestly writer himself as the father of more than the Judahites. Not only was he the ancestor of the ten tribes of Israel to the north of Judah, but also of Ishmael and Jacob's brother Esau, who fathered a whole set of non-Israelite peoples. Although in later times and writings the covenant of Abraham involving circumcision was taken to signify a unique identity for the Jew, for the priestly writer it could not possibly have had this meaning. He had something else in mind.

Why was the ritual of circumcision practiced?[1] Historically, reproductive rituals in general may be understood as "political tactics used to solve social dilemmas that become crucial at certain points in the human reproductive cycle."[2] "Reproductive rituals are attempts to gain political advantage in conflicts over women and children. . . . [They are] motivated by self-interest; their sentimental and religious symbolism merely cloaks their true objectives." Public political rituals represent "political bargaining tactics for defending claims, influencing public opinion, and monitoring the intentions of potential competitors."[3]

In the ancient world, political power was dependent on the number of males who were available to defend the clan. Political power and reproductive potency went hand in hand. The order to "be fruitful

1. This question has received many answers. From a historical perspective, the recent discussion of Paige and Paige provides the best answer currently available. See Karen Ericksen Paige and Jeffery M. Paige, *The Politics of Reproductive Ritual* (Berkeley: University of California Press, 1981), especially 122–66.
2. Ibid., 43.
3. Ibid., 50.

and multiply" in the priestly creation story "typifies the political thought not only of the Hebrew patriarchs but of men in most strong fraternal interest group societies. . . . Since military power and political power depend on the continual expansion of the number of males in the clans, strong fraternal interest groups place an overwhelming value on fecundity."[4]

But there is an inherent tension in the desire to generate more sons in order to increase the clan's political power. The more sons a man has, the greater the likelihood that the larger family will benefit from some kind of separation of resources, with the accompanying crisis of loyalty and cohesion. "In societies with strong fraternal interest groups . . . the fissioning of adult family heads can radically upset the existing balance of power by altering the political structure of a major lineage or clan."[5] Will the family hold together and thus keep intact the original family's power, or will it fission into separate units?

The dilemma solved by circumcision is precisely this crisis of loyalty that arises when a son becomes old enough to establish his own family in a society where political power depends on maintaining strong fraternal interest groups, or extensive networks of loyal kin under the control of a dominant head. Circumcision is a surveillance ritual, a means of making certain of the loyalty of sons to the clan.

In traditional societies, circumcision was and is always performed in the presence of the males of the wider family, who watch the proceedings carefully. "They gain visible public evidence that the head of a family unit of their lineage is willing to trust others with his and his family's most valuable political asset, his son's penis. If the surgeon's hands are unsteady, they may gain castration or even death [through bleeding or infection], thus eliminating a competitive and potentially fissionable segment within the primary lineage." But the elimination of potential competition is not the immediate objective of the ritual. Its immediate purpose is to foster loyalty:

> If the operation is successful, both sides gain a certain degree of satisfaction. The lineage elders have the satisfaction of knowing that, whatever a given father's future plans for lineage fission, he is sufficiently loyal to his kin to publicly expose the source of his future political power to danger. The father, while resenting the

4. Ibid., 127.
5. Ibid., 125.

risk to his son, can expect under normal circumstances to gain the continued trust of his consanguineal kin and to retain the reproductive power of his son. The behavior of father, son, and consanguineal kin during the ceremony provides valuable information both to the father and, more importantly, to his influential elder kinsmen. Like other ceremonies, the circumcision ceremony allows a man both to assess and to influence the opinions of important political allies or enemies.[6]

In sum, "a circumcision ceremony is a surveillance ritual by which members of a strong fraternal interest group, particularly the most influential members, assess and minimize the likelihood of fission by requiring a public demonstration of loyalty of any man who has a son."[7]

The timing of circumcision varies widely from society to society, from infancy to early adulthood. But two elements are common to all known circumcision ceremonies: the ritual always takes place before the marriage of the man, the critical event that presents the dilemma that circumcision is designed to address; and it is always carried out under the scrutiny of the father's consanguineal kinsmen.

MORE BLOOD

While this was likely the underlying reason for practicing circumcision, it does not tell us about the Aaronid priesthood's own understanding of the practice. What did the priests have in mind when they rationalized an important existing practice and placed it within the framework of the priestly world?

Blood is the element that holds the life of all creatures that move in God's created order. The disposition of blood—the control of the discharge and flow of blood—may be regarded as a virtual obsession with the Aaronid priesthood. It happens, however, that the female of the species experiences a flow of blood that can be quite uncontrolled, and which flows from her reproductive parts during the very period of her life when she is able to reproduce whenever she is not already involved with reproduction through pregnancy and nursing.

6. Ibid., 147–48.
7. Ibid., 148–9.

At such times she is regarded as not fulfilling the injunction to "be fruitful and multiply," and is therefore unclean.[8]

This apparent irregularity suggested to the minds of males, already dominant in the public arena of Judahite culture, that females are less in tune with God's creation than males. Consequently the woman's normal flow of blood was treated as an impurity:

> When a woman has a discharge of blood which is her regular discharge from her body, she shall be in her impurity for seven days, and whoever touches her shall be unclean until the evening [i.e., for the rest of that day]. (Lev. 15:19, RSV)

This impurity was severe enough to infect everything the woman came into contact with:

> And everything upon which she lies during her impurity shall be unclean; everything also upon which she sits shall be unclean. And whoever touches her bed shall wash his clothes, and bathe himself in water, and be unclean until the evening. And whoever touches anything upon which she sits shall wash his clothes, and bathe himself in water, and be unclean until the evening; whether it is the bed or anything upon which she sits, when he touches it he shall be unclean until the evening. And if any man lies with her, and her impurity is on him, he shall be unclean seven days; and every bed on which he lies shall be unclean.

In some cases a woman discharged blood abnormally:

> If a woman has a discharge of blood for many days, not at the time of her impurity, or if she has a discharge beyond the time of her impurity, all the days of the discharge she shall continue in un-cleanness; as in the days of her impurity, she shall be unclean.

This situation called for an offering for "sin" no less, in order to expiate for the supposed violation of the created order:

> If she is cleansed of her discharge, she shall count for herself seven days, and after that she shall be clean. And on the eighth day she

---

8. As often pointed out, in the ancient world menses probably occupied only a short part of the fertile portion of a woman's life. "Menstruation as we know it today is largely a product of contraception and of an increase in the number of childbearing years. Until this century, most women spent the years between their first menses around the age of 14 and their menopause at age 35 or 40 either pregnant or breastfeeding." See Robin Marantz Henig, "Dispelling Menstrual Myths," *New York Times Magazine,* March 7, 1982, 65, cited in Mayer I. Gruber, "Women in the Cult, According to the Priestly Code," in Jacob Neusner, ed., *Judaic Perspectives on Ancient Israel* (Philadelphia: Fortress Press, 1987), 47; Gordon J. Wenham, *The Book of Leviticus* (Grand Rapids: William B. Eerdmans, 1979), 223–24.

shall take two turtledoves or two young pigeons, and bring them
to the priest, to the door of the tent of meeting [tabernacle]. And
the priest shall offer one for a sin offering and the other for a whole
burnt offering, and so make satisfaction for her before Yahweh for
her unclean discharge.

Thus you shall keep the people of Israel demarcated from their
uncleanness, lest they die in their uncleanness by defiling my tabernacle. (Lev. 15:20-30, RSV, with minor changes)

A man may also discharge blood, pus, or semen, and so become
similarly unclean, and the man's case is actually presented before the
woman's in Leviticus 15. But since it was the woman who was marked
out as subject to such a discharge as a matter of course, she was
regarded as the lesser of the two sexes in the hierarchy of degrees of
congruence with the created order. All humans are created in the
image of God, but some are nearer the image than others, since no
doubt God, in the priestly view, does not suffer involuntary discharges
of blood.

The taboo of menstruation was of course not unique to the Judahites. "While the menstrual taboo is cultically defined and regulated,
it is so universal a factor of human culture that it may be viewed as
a general social concept apart from its specific interpretation and in-
stitutionalization in the Israelite cultus."[9] Nevertheless, the perception
of menstruation as unclean had profound implications for the organization of the priestly world of the cult.

LIMITS ON WOMEN

Not the least of these was that the cult was a male institution, and
the priesthood exclusively male. Under the priestly regime, "women,
who were disenfranchised in the political realm, were disenfranchised
in the religious realm as well."[10] The male privilege of the priesthood
is specified in the second covenant in the priestly tradition, the covenant of Abraham, which relates to the reproductive parts and to their
flows of blood. The sign of the second covenant is circumcision, in
which the male reproductive part is made to discharge blood in a
male-controlled rather than uncontrollable procedure. This privilege

---

9. Phyllis Bird, "The Place of Women in the Israelite Cultus," in *Ancient Israelite Religion: Essays
in Honor of Frank Moore Cross,* ed. Patrick D. Miller, Paul D. Hanson, and S. Dean McBride
(Philadelphia: Fortress Press, 1987), 414, footnote 21.
10. Ibid., 397.

in relation to the female's flow of blood establishes the priority and all other privileges of the male in general.

While religious participation must be defined more widely than the official priestly cult, and in such a wider concept of religious participation women played a significant role, it remains true that in ancient Israel there was a "congruence of military, legal, and cultic assemblies; the three represent the primary institutions of the public sphere, which is everywhere the sphere of male activity."[11]

> Leadership of the cultus appears at all times to have been in the hands of males (though with differing patterns and sources of recruitment into the leadership group). Women, however, were not excluded absolutely from cultic service or sacred space, though increasing restriction is suggested, correlated with increasing centralization, specialization, and power (at least in Judah) under a royally sanctioned Zadokite priesthood.[12]

In the narrative of the priestly scrolls, circumcision, the sign of the second covenant, was instituted following the giving of the sign of the first covenant, the bow and the eating of flesh it sanctioned. Similarly, in the elaboration of ritual cleanness as part of the comprehensive law of the third covenant, circumcision (Leviticus 12) is treated directly after meat eating (Leviticus 11). Here the greater cleanness of males is made explicit:

> If a woman conceives and bears a male child, then she shall be unclean seven [7] days; as at the time of her menstruation, she shall be unclean. And on the eighth day, the flesh of his foreskin shall be circumcised. Then she shall continue for thirty-three $[10 \times 3 + 3]$ days in the blood of her purifying; she shall not touch any holy thing, nor come into the sanctuary, until the days of her purifying are completed. If she bears a female child, then she shall be unclean fourteen days, as in her menstruation; and she shall continue in the blood of her purifying for sixty-six days. (Lev. 12:2-5, RSV)

In plain words, the male is twice as clean as the female. The redemption price for women is hence a half or three-fifths that of men.

11. Ibid., 403.
12. Ibid., 405. See also Gruber, "Women in the Cult According to the Priestly Code," 35–48. Gruber's essay argues that the exclusion of women may be overstated by modern scholars. Women participated in Israelite cults in limited ways; that they played subordinate roles in the dominant public cults is irrefutable.

This set of perceptions, values, and procedures is what is anticipated in the second covenant, the covenant of Abraham with its sign of circumcision, in the overture to Israel's abundant multiplication:

> God said to Abram, "I am El Shadday; walk before me, and be blameless. I will make my covenant between me and you, and will multiply you exceedingly." Abram fell on his face; and God said to him, "My covenant is with you, and you shall be the father of a multitude of nations. No longer shall your name be Abram,[13] but your name shall be Abraham;[14] for I have made you the father of a multitude of nations. I will make you exceedingly fruitful; and I will make nations of you, and kings shall come forth from you. And I will establish my covenant between me and you and your descendants after you throughout their generations for an everlasting covenant. . . . And I will give to you and to your descendants after you the land of your sojourning, all the land of Canaan, for an everlasting possession. . . .
>
> This is my covenant which you shall keep, between me and you and your descendants after you: every male among you shall be circumcised. You shall be circumcised in the flesh of your foreskins, and it shall be a sign of the covenant between me and you. . . . So shall my covenant be in your flesh an everlasting covenant. (Gen. 17:1-13, RSV, with slight changes)

This second covenant goes on to involve Sarah, the second member of the human sexual pair through whom the creation command to be fruitful and multiply is fulfilled. Sarah receives attention comparable to Abraham's, at least to the point of receiving a new name (and further if the ostensibly improbable view that El *Shadday* refers to breasts turns out to be correct):

> God said to Abraham, "As for Sarai your wife, you shall not call her name Sarai, but Sarah shall be her name. I will bless her, and moreover I will give you a son by her; I will bless her, and she shall be a mother of nations; kings of peoples shall come from her."

This attention to Sarah does not mean that the priestly writer regarded the sexes as equal. It goes without saying that both sexes play an essential role in reproduction. However, it is a misunderstanding of the view of the priestly writer to imagine that, just because

---

13. Meaning something like "the father is high."
14. Understood to mean "father of a multitude."

Genesis 1 refers to the creation of both male and female in the image of God, and Abraham and Sarah receive similar attention in the account of the covenant of circumcision, male and female enjoy an equality in the sight of God.

These parts of the priestly tradition, then, are the texts that help us to understand the part of the account of creation that deals with human beings:

> So God created humans in his own image, in the image of God he created them; male and female he created them. And God blessed them, and God said to them, "Be fruitful and multiply, and fill the earth and subdue it; and have dominion over the fish of the sea and over the birds of the air and over every living thing that moves upon the earth."

The focus placed on circumcision by the priestly writer, and its relation to his account of creation, fits with his forceful and controlled presentation of a cultically and militarily united Israelite people, drawn together through bonds of mutual loyalty to the covenants of Noah, Abraham, and Moses, as though Israel were one huge fraternal interest group to which a man's loyalty was of utmost importance. In the priestly conception seen in Exodus and Numbers, Israel moves and camps in military formation. This view also fits with the basic meaning of the sacrifices as tribute to the system of polity and jurisdiction represented by the temple in Jerusalem.

8

How We Got Our
Work Week

As the introduction to the priestly reinterpretation of the official temple history, the creation story of Genesis 1 represents a small but essential base, as though a pyramid were turned upside down to rest on its point. The introduction must be understood in terms of the themes it points to in the rest of the priestly tradition. The themes of particular interest in the first place are the three practices that serve as signs for the three covenants.

THE PRIESTLY SABBATH

Although they may not understand its meaning, many in our culture are familiar with the sign of the first covenant, not eating certain meats. They at least know that strict practitioners of Jewish custom do not eat pork. The sign of the second covenant, circumcision, is also familiar, since it is widely practiced in the United States, although not for religious reasons. The sign of the third covenant, the Sabbath, is even more well known. People are familiar with the Jewish day of Sabbath rest, the Christian "Sabbath" on the first day of the week, Sabbath laws, witches' Sabbaths, and sabbatical leaves. Because it is introduced explicitly in the well-known creation story in the first chapter of Genesis, many are even aware that the Sabbath is the basis of the seven-day week in our culture:

> When on the seventh day God had finished his work which he had done, he rested on the seventh day from all his work which he had done. So God blessed the seventh day and made it holy, because

on it God rested from all his work which he had done in creation. (Gen. 2:2-3).

The word "Sabbath" does not actually occur here. The Hebrew verb translated "rest," however, is *shabat*, from which the word *shabbat*, "Sabbath," was thought to derive. The verb *shabat* means to cease or desist. To cease work is to rest. Every reader of the priestly story of creation would have known the Sabbath was being alluded to. When the Sabbath is prescribed later in the priestly revision of the official history of Israel, there is immediate reference back to the seventh day of creation.

We take the week for granted. It is not, however, a natural unit of time. The day, month, and year are based on the manifest behavior of the sun and moon. They were thus already implicit by the end of the fourth day of creation. As units of time they are widely attested in the cultures of humanity. In contrast, the fixed week, intermediate between the day and the month, does not correspond directly to any recurring event in the sky and is a more or less arbitrary unit of time. The week as we know it has seven days, though other lengths have been possible. The seven-day week in Western culture comes from the Bible, from the priestly revision in the Tetrateuch. Although there were influences on this priestly tradition, as far as is known it was essentially thought up by the priests of Jerusalem in the sixth century B.C.E.

Because the Bible leaves a person with the understanding that the Sabbath was established at the beginning as a day of rest, it requires effort to imagine that the Sabbath as the priestly writer presents it was a new concept in the sixth century B.C.E., and that the seven-day week was unknown prior to the Babylonian or early Persian period in Israel, after most of the Old Testament had already been written.

THE SABBATH BEFORE P

The concept of rest days, or Sabbaths, had been known from early times in Israel. But prior to the sixth century, the term Sabbath may have had quite a different meaning from the meaning given it in Genesis 1 and the rest of the priestly history. This apparently is why, whenever he is talking about the Sabbath, the priestly writer states repeatedly that he means "the seventh day," as though he were trying to drive home an unfamiliar point.

The day of rest called Sabbath that existed in Israel before the time of the priestly writer probably did not fall every seven days, but on the full moon—once every 29 days on average. When texts from the period of the monarchy, before the time of the priestly writer, speak about the Sabbath, they are referring to a periodic day of rest and cult feasting during which buying and selling were sometimes discouraged. The Akkadian cognate *shabattu* means both the full moon and the day of the full moon. Hebrew *shabbat* is used in parallelism with *kese'*, which also means the full moon. For instance, in the ninth century B.C.E., the rich woman of Shunem wanted to fetch Elisha to save her son. Her husband, not knowing her purpose, answered, "Why will you go to him today? It is neither new moon nor *sabbath*" (2 Kings 4:23). In the eighth century, Amos denounced the wealthy of Samaria when they griped, "When will the new moon be over, that we may sell grain? And the *sabbath*, that we may offer wheat for sale?" (Amos 8:5). Not long after, Hosea denounced the celebrations of the elite in Israel in these words: "I will put an end to all her mirth, her feasts, her new moons, her *sabbaths*, and all her appointed feasts" (Hos. 2:11). At the same time, Isaiah, quoting God, referred to the sacrificial aspect of such feasts:

> What to me is the multitude of your sacrifices? I have had enough of burnt offerings of rams and the fat of fed beasts; I do not delight in the blood of bulls, or of lambs, or of he-goats. When you come to appear before me, who requires of you this trampling of my courts? Bring no more vain offerings; incense is an abomination to me. New moon and *sabbath* and the calling of assemblies—I cannot endure iniquity and solemn assembly. (Isa. 1:11-13, RSV)

Historians have seen in these uses of the word Sabbath references to a modest feast day celebrated at various local shrines, for some people involving a short pilgrimage and sacrifices. The feast is yoked with the new moon, suggesting that the Sabbath designated, as in Akkadian, the full moon. The assumption in the priestly history that the early spring and fall harvest feasts should always fall simultaneously on the fifteenth of the lunar month and on a Sabbath—an impossibility—is a further vestige of the same meaning.

WHY SEVEN DAYS?

For the priests, however, the Sabbath recurred in a seven-day cycle. How did the idea of a seventh-day Sabbath develop and come to replace the full-moon Sabbath? Where did the priestly writer get his concept of the seven-day week?[1]

There was nothing in Palestine's tradition suggesting that a seven-day period had ever previously been a calendrical unit.[2] The priests did not borrow the seven-day scheme from somewhere else in particular, but devised it from elements that were to be found elsewhere, particularly under Babylonian influence in the sixth century B.C.E.

One text referring to such a unit of time has been known for over a hundred years. It was discovered during the ongoing excavation of Assurbanipal's library in Nineveh in 1869. It attests Assyrian usage in the seventh century B.C.E.[3] The text is an omen calendar, comprising a list of days and activities, along with a designation of each day as auspicious or inauspicious ("evil"), or both. The inauspicious days are the 7th, 14th, 21st, and 28th, and the 19th. Why the 19th? The most likely explanation is that it marks the day in a following month that is 7x7, or 49, days from the first of the preceding month. The activities discouraged in this calendar from the royal palace apply to the king alone. "On the five specified days, the king is not, for instance, to eat food prepared by fire, not to put on royal dress or offer sacrifice, not to ride in his chariot, or hold court, not to seek an oracle, or even to invoke curses on his enemies."[4] Although these days are not called Sabbaths and hardly represent a seven-day week, since the cycle does not run continuously but must start over again at the beginning of each lunar month, they attest the practice of dividing time into cycles of seven days.

It is of interest that texts from the ancient world describe the construction of temples in periods of seven days. Examples are Gudea's temple in Lagash in a text from the twenty-second century B.C.E.,

1. This question has occupied historians for a century or more, without a definitive answer emerging. Too little is known about the Sabbath in Israel and in neighboring cultures during the centuries prior to the composition of the priestly revision of the temple history. More information could emerge at any time through archaeology. For the present, the explanation suggested here may be the most likely interpretation of what evidence does exist. See particularly André Lemaire, "Le sabbat a l'époque royale israélite," *Revue biblique* 80 (1973): 161–85.
2. It will be argued later that several references to a seven-day Sabbath prior to P, particularly Exod. 23:12, 34:21, and Deut. 5:13-14, resulted from priestly revisions of the Torah and mixing of texts. Historians are not of one mind on this matter.
3. The precise bearing of this text on the patterning of the Sabbath in Judahite priestly circles is not clear, but most historians believe that the tradition it indicates had some kind of influence.
4. *A Dictionary of the Bible*, ed. James Hastings (Edinburgh: T. & T. Clark, 1902), vol. 4, p. 319. For a translation of the text, see Morris Jastrow, *The Religion of Babylonia and Assyria* (Boston: Ginn & Company, 1898), 373–78.

and Baal's temple at Ugarit in a text from the fourteenth century. But the closest parallels to the priestly seven-day period come from Mesopotamia, in texts dating just before the time of the priestly writer.[5] The account of the creation of the world in the fifth tablet of the *Enuma elish* shows that at least some people in ancient Mesopotamia thought of the phases of the moon in terms of seven-day periods:

> The moon he caused to shine, the night to him entrusting. He appointed him a creature of the night to signify the days: "Monthly, without cease, form designs with a crown. At the month's very start, rising over the land, you shall have luminous horns to signify six days, on the seventh day reaching a half-crown. At full moon stand in opposition in mid-month. When the sun overtakes you at the base of the sky, diminish your crown and retrogress in light. At the time of disappearance approach the course of the sun, and on the twenty-ninth you shall again stand in opposition to the sun."[6]

The lunar month is 29½ days, so seven days is the nearest quarter in whole days. Yet after only a month or two, a seven-day cycle no longer matches the lunar cycle. The notion of seven in this text results from rationalizing the phases of the moon in a way that is not in itself useful for designing a calendar.

Although we do not have detailed information on the priests' understanding of astronomy and the calendar, we know the idea that

5. There is a venerable scholarly tradition of comparing the Mesopotamian texts with the Bible in order to elucidate the biblical Sabbath, though scholars differ on the usefulness of these comparisons. See Niels-Erik A. Andreasen, *The Old Testament Sabbath* (Missoula: Society of Biblical Literature, 1972). Andreasen is somewhat skeptical of such comparisons. William H. Hallo, "New Moons and Sabbaths: A Case-Study in the Contrastive Approach," *Hebrew Union College Annual* 48 (1977): 1–18, appears to have made the most recent thorough collection and judicious interpretation of the evidence. In the instance of the Sabbath, Hallo prefers to stress the contrast between biblical Israel and the ancient Near East, and so is disinclined to admit any Mesopotamian influence at all on the origin of the Sabbath. Thus he downplays the evidence for a lunar feast calendar in monarchic Israel, assumes that the word Sabbath referred to a seven-day cycle in all biblical texts regardless of date or possible textual mixing, and disregards the probable dating and social context of biblical texts, particularly those composed in their present form by the exilic and Persian-period priests of Jerusalem. Despite the thoroughness and usefulness of his research, Hallo does not seem to have noted Lemaire's article, the basic results of which are followed here. The issue is not whether Israelites borrowed the Sabbath from Mesopotamians; it seems clear they did not. The issue is whether the Israelite priests who composed the priestly history were at all influenced by Mesopotamian tradition in their formulation of the seven-day week; it seems equally clear that they were. It is likely that Lemaire's restatement of some of the older views represents the most accurate summary of the current state of knowledge. See Lemaire, "Le sabbat a l'époque royale israélite."

6. Tablet 5, lines 12-18; see James B. Pritchard, *Ancient Near Eastern Texts Relating to the Old Testament*, 2d ed. (Princeton: Princeton University Press, 1955), 68.

the heavenly lights should govern the calendar was not foreign to them.[7] Indeed, it is stated explicitly in the creation story itself: "Let there be lights in the firmament of the heavens to separate the day from the night; and let them be for signs and for periods and for days and years" (Gen. 1:14). While the basic unit of time—the seven-day cycle—created by the priests appears to be based on the phases of the moon, that this agreed with the existence of exactly seven moving heavenly lights (the seven planets) must have struck them as confirmation of their reassignment of the Sabbath to every seventh day.

An apparent coincidence turned the day of Sabbath into the "day of El" not long after the priestly formulation of the seven-day week. Next to Yahweh, El was the god of most interest to the priestly writer.[8] In the Greek and Egyptian cultural spheres during the later Hellenistic period, the Greek ordering of the seven planets and Egyptian division of the day into twenty-four hours were combined to assign each of the seven days of the Jewish week to a particular planet and its god. This assignment can still be seen in the names of the days in English and many other languages, in which the seventh day is called Saturday, standing for the day of Saturn, or El.

The Greek list of planets ran according to their apparent distance from Earth, which was calculated by how long it took each to move through the Zodiac once: Saturn-Jupiter-Mars-Sun-Venus-Mercury-Moon. A given day was assigned to the planet of its first hour. The first hour of the first day belonged to the Sun by definition. Thus the first day was called Sun's day, or Sunday in English. The second hour of the first day belonged to Venus, the third hour to Mercury, the fourth to the Moon, the fifth to Saturn, and so forth through the list and back again until the twenty-fourth, which ended up belonging to Mercury. (Why? Figure it out.)[9] This meant the first hour of the second day belonged to the planet immediately following Mercury in the list, or the Moon. Hence the second day was called Moon's day—Monday in English, *lundi* in French (from Latin *luna,* "moon"). This scheme was followed all the way through the week. Tuesday was Mars's day, Wednesday Mercury's, Thursday Jupiter's and Friday

7. Many attempts have been made to relate the seven moving heavenly bodies, the "planets" (including sun and moon), to the seven-day week, as they were related during the Hellenistic period and later, but historians have not generally found these attempts convincing.
8. See below, chapter 9.
9. Every seventh hour—the first, eighth, fifteenth, and twenty-second—of the first day would belong to the Sun, the twenty-third hour to Venus, the twenty-fourth to Mercury.

Venus's. The English weekday names came from the equivalent Germanic deities: Mars was Tiwaz, or Tiu, Mercury was Woden, Jupiter was Thor, and Venus was Frija.

In this scheme, the seventh day or Sabbath was Saturn's day—Saturday, or Kronos's day in Greek, since Roman Saturn was Greek Kronos. In the comparison of Roman and Greek with Semitic theology, Saturn and Kronos, the divine patriarchs, were equivalent to El. In this scheme, therefore, which quickly prevailed wherever the Jewish and Christian calendar was used in the Mediterranean and Eastern world, the Sabbath was El's day. This designation matched Jewish priestly theory perfectly. It probably did not, however, originate with the Jewish priests behind the priestly history: the Persian order of the planets differed from the Greek order; the Egyptian pattern of twenty-four hours was not used in the Persian world before the Hellenistic period; and, of course, the Jewish priests would have regarded all days as belonging equally to the one God.

The week as we know it was an invention of the sixth-century B.C.E. priesthood of Jerusalem. In time the Sabbath-based week became a part of Christian practice, then Roman and Byzantine, until it spread throughout Western culture.[10]

In a striking manner, the priests dissociated the Sabbath from the lunar cycle. Probably under Babylonian influence, the priestly writers took an aspect of the Babylonian lunar month as represented in Babylonian creation tradition—the seven-day phases of the moon—abstracted or divorced this seven-day unit from the lunar month, and reassigned the term *shabbat* to it on the basis of an etymological understanding of *shabbat* as referring to the "cessation" of work.[11]

There is nothing new about etymologizing in the Bible. It is done in many documents as a matter of course. It is not historical etymologies that are meant, but word similarities that suggested to the ancient ear the derivation or "true meaning" of a word. Examples of priestly etymologizing or re-etymologizing are several. Characteristic of the priestly history is the taking of some archaic term and giving it a new meaning through verbal relations. Abraham, a variant of the name Abram, was taken by the priestly writer to mean "father of a

---

10. F. H. Colson, *The Week: An Essay on the Origin and Development of the Seven-Day Cycle* (Cambridge: Cambridge University Press, 1926); Hallo, "New Moons and Sabbaths."
11. This may have been the historical etymology of the term. See M. Tsevat, "The Basic Meaning of the Biblical Sabbath," *Zeitschrift für die alttestamentliche Wissenschaft* 84 (1972): 447–59.

broad multitude," in line with the priestly command to be fruitful and multiply. *Shakan,* used cultically to mean "to place" or "set" the name of God at a particular location, is re-analyzed to mean "to tent" or "tabernacle," in line with the primacy of the cultic *mishkan,* or "tent." *'Edut,* "covenant," is an interpretation of an archaic term for covenant stipulations whose meaning changes in the conception of the priestly writer in relation with the tent of *mo'ed,* "meeting, covenant."[12]

The point, then, is not that there were no periods based on seven before the time of the priestly writers, but that they related all these to creation by abstracting the seven-day scheme as an absolute from the lunar cycle and then relating the traditional periods of seven to this new Sabbath scheme. The priests' interest in the number seven, which for them is a corollary of the Sabbath, extends to other practices. The ordination of priests and the consecration of the altar last seven days (Exod. 29:35-37). Sacrificial blood is sprinkled seven times (Lev. 4:6, 17; 14:7; 16:4). The anointing oil is sprinkled seven times (Lev. 8:11). A seven-branch lampstand adorns the cult. According to P, seventy Israelites went to Egypt in the time of Joseph (Exod. 1:5).

What led the priests to redefine the Sabbath in terms of an abstracted Babylonian cultural artifact? It is likely the Judahite priestly tradition was in line with a Persian practice inherited from the Babylonians.[13] Lists of monthly sacrifices from Uruk in Babylonia in the Persian period prescribe the *hitpu* offering for the 7th, 14th, 21st, and 28th days of the month. The Persian month, however, continued to be a lunar month, and thus these sacrifices did not follow a calendar based on the week. That was uniquely Judean.

THE SABBATH AND PRIESTLY RULE

Through the novel scheme of observing Sabbaths every seven days instead of on the full moon, the priests increased the number of Sabbathlike feast days possibly as much as fourfold. This strengthened their position as elites who were privileged to consume meat on a

12. Frank M. Cross, *Canaanite Myth and Hebrew Epic* (Cambridge: Harvard University Press, 1973), 312–13, 322; Delbert R. Hillers, *Covenant: The History of a Biblical Idea* (Baltimore: Johns Hopkins Press, 1969), 160–64.
13. See Hallo, "New Moons and Sabbaths," 8–9. Hallo dismisses the relevance of these texts for understanding the biblical Sabbath because of their use in former times to argue for a simple Babylonian origin of the Sabbath, based on the erroneous equation of the Sabbath with Babylonian lunar cycles.

regular basis, since the Sabbath was the occasion for leisure and specifically for the *shelem* sacrifice that represented a meal in which the
priest might join.[14] The conclusion of the Sabbath prescription in
Exodus 31:17, "and God was refreshed," likely refers not only to rest
but to the restoration of the *nephesh* through partaking of food (see
also Exod. 23:12). The Aaronid priesthood in this way increased the
frequency of ceremony in Persian Judah and hence the investment of
the villagers' ceremonial fund in the priestly cult and its jurisdiction.
The peasants might sometimes have ignored the priests' theory of
times and sacrifices, but their livestock was channeled into the cult
in any case, whether as tax, tribute, gift, or ransom.

In the Persian period the Sabbath became especially important to
the ideal of priestly rule. It appears added to, or reinterpreted in, the
book of Jeremiah (Jer. 17:19-27). It is made the basis of loyalty and
obedience to the just law of Moses in the collection of oracles that
concludes the book of Isaiah (Isaiah 56–66), which probably represents
the view of a Levitical group of priests in the mid-fifth century, around
the time of Nehemiah (Isa. 56:2, 4, 6; 63:13; 66:23). In Nehemiah it
becomes an essential feature of the Persian attempt to regain control
over local trade in Judah (Nehemiah 13). It may have been part of
the Persian attempt to control trade when it was first instituted through
the priesthood in the sixth century B.C.E.

THE SABBATH IN P

In revising the official temple history of Israel, why did the priestly
writer lay such stress on the reconceived seventh-day Sabbath? The
most obvious reason was to enforce the observance of what was in
effect a new practice, the observance of a weekly Sabbath. To accom-
plish this, the priestly writer used the Sabbath to tie his work together
and thus tighten the sense of completeness and wholeness that it
conveys. In the priestly work, all aspects of history and cult relate to
creation, the primary events that fixed the orders of the created
world.[15] The way things are—with the priestly cult at the center of

14. Lemaire, "Le sabbat," 185: "A l'époque royale, la célébration du sabbat consistait essentielle-
ment dans le rassemblement des Israélites dans les divers sanctuaires du pays pour l'offrande de
sacrifices, holocaustes et sacrifices 'pacifiques', dans une atmosphère de fête."
15. See for example Peter J. Kearney, "Creation and Liturgy: The P Redaction of Ex. 25–40,"
Zeitschrift für die alttestamentliche Wissenschaft 89 (1977): 375–87. Kearney shows that the composition
of Exod. 25–31 follows an outline derived from the account of creation in Gen. 1:1—2:3. See
also M. Barnouin, "Les recensements du livre des Nombres et l'astronomie babylonienne," *Vetus*

space, time, status, and acceptability—is grounded in the stability, finality, and inevitability of the self-contained priestly construction of historical reality. In this sense the Sabbath is at the heart of the priestly ideal.

A second reason the priestly writer laid such stress on the seven-day cycle was to allow him to fit his analysis of life, movement, and meat into the traditional division of the universe into the three realms of sea, sky, and earth. The creation of these three realms is described as occurring in three days, then in a further three days they are re-iterated as the realms of three kinds of moving creatures, for a total of six days. The seventh follows on this scheme as a settled matter of course.

Although the Sabbath theme recurs at significant intervals through-out the priestly history, together with allusions and references back to the creation account, it is often not realized that outside the priestly portions of scripture, the Sabbath is dealt with little in the Old Testament. Most of the references later than the priestly revision occur in just three places: Jeremiah 17, Isaiah 56 and 66, and Nehemiah 13. All these refer themselves to the priestly concept of Sabbath. In Third Isaiah, for example, the Sabbath stands for the fuller collection of the laws of Moses, just as it does in the priestly work. Besides these, there is only a handful of references to Sabbath left.

EXODUS

The importance the priests placed on their reconception of Sabbath is evidenced by the fact that they made it the sign of the third eternal covenant. Following the establishment of the seven-day week in the creation story, the priestly writer refrains from making reference to the Sabbath until after the introduction of the third covenant in the time of Moses (Exodus 6). The first reference does occur, though, before the writer announces that the Sabbath is the sign of the third covenant. He introduces the Sabbath into the story of how Israel was fed with manna in the wilderness in words reminiscent of the account of creation:

> On the sixth day they gathered twice as much bread, two omers apiece; and when all the leaders of the congregation came and told

Testamentum 27 (1977): 280–303. The following statement sums up Barnouin's point incisively: "The priestly traditions have idealised the narrative of the desert. They have enriched it with quantities of precisions pertaining to the liturgical ritual and the calendar in a manner which presents Israel as a people whose sacred religion unifies them and ties them to God for all time" (*Old Testament Abstracts* 1:2 [June 1978]: 155–56).

Moses, he said to them, "This is what Yahweh has commanded: 'Tomorrow is a solemn Sabbath, a holy Sabbath to Yahweh; bake what you will bake and boil what you will boil, and all that is left over lay by to be kept until the morning.' " So they laid it by until morning. . . . Moses said, "Eat it today, for today is a Sabbath to Yahweh; today you will not find it in the field. *Six days you shall gather it; but on the seventh day, which is a Sabbath, there will be none.* . . . Yahweh has given you the Sabbath, therefore on the sixth day he gives you bread for two days; remain every one at home, let no one go out on the seventh day." So the people rested (*shabath*) on the seventh day. (Exod. 16:22-30, RSV slightly modified and shortened)

By placing his first mention of the Sabbath on the heels of God's deliverance of Israel from Egypt, the priestly writer was making use of a tradition familiar to the priests of the sixth century B.C.E. concerning the relief of workers, including slaves and animals, from work—a tradition said by the temple scriptures to date back to God's deliverance of the Israelite workers from hard labor in Egypt. By linking the Sabbath to this tradition, the priestly writer was directly relating the observance of the Sabbath to the central theme of the original official temple history of Israel—the deliverance of forced laborers from Egypt—as illustrated in Deuteronomy:

Observe the Sabbath day, to keep it holy. . . . You shall remember that you were a slave in the land of Egypt, and *Yahweh your God brought you out from there with a mighty hand and an outstretched arm; therefore Yahweh your God commanded you to keep the Sabbath day.* (Deut. 5:12-15)

The elaboration of this meaning of Sabbath is withheld until later in the priestly work. For the time being the writer is much more interested in the concept of the Sabbath as the seventh day of creation.

The next reference to the Sabbath, in the Exodus version of the Ten Commandments, gives a different reason for resting from the one just cited from Deuteronomy. It relates it instead to creation:

Remember the Sabbath day, to keep it holy. Six days you shall labor, and do all your work; but the seventh day is a Sabbath to Yahweh your God; in it you shall not do any work, you, or your son, or your daughter, or your male or female slave, or your cattle, or the resident alien who is within your gates; *for in six days Yahweh made heaven and earth, the sea, and all that is in them, and rested on the seventh day; therefore Yahweh blessed the Sabbath day and made it holy.* (Exod. 20:8-11)[16]

Here the word for rest is not *shabat,* but a more common word for rest (*nah*). The priestly understanding of *shabat* as rest is thereby made clear. In Exodus 23:12, both words are used, although this is not apparent in the RSV, which translates both as "rest."

This meaning of *shabat* is even more clear in the next reference to Sabbath in the priestly work, which is placed in an important position in relation to the structure of the priestly narrative. Coming at the conclusion of the priestly law concerning the tabernacle and its cultic apparatus, and the naming of Bezalel and Oholiab as the chief craftsmen for carrying out these instructions, it is the main statement of the Sabbath law and describes the Sabbath as the sign of the third covenant:

> Yahweh said to Moses, "Say to the people of Israel, 'You shall keep my Sabbaths, for this is a *sign* between me and you throughout your generations, that you may know that I, Yahweh, make you holy. You shall keep the Sabbath, because it is holy for you; every one who profanes it shall be put to death; whoever does any work on it, that person shall be cut off from among their people. *Six days shall work be done, but the seventh day is a Sabbath of a solemn Sabbath [cessation], holy to Yahweh;* whoever does any work on the Sabbath day shall be put to death. Wherefore the people of Israel shall keep the Sabbath, observing the Sabbath throughout their generations, as an eternal covenant. It is a *sign* forever between me and the people of Israel that *in six days Yahweh made heaven and earth, and on the seventh day he rested [shabat], and was refreshed.* (Exod. 31:12-17, RSV, slightly modified)

At just this point, Yahweh presents Moses with the two stone slabs on which the ten commandments were inscribed with the finger of God and sends him back to his people. Exodus 32, 33, and 34 may be bracketed, as they are earlier than the priestly writer's revision of the official temple history. When the priestly writer resumes his lengthy contribution to the story of Israel at Sinai, which runs more

16. The reference to the seventh day is here assumed to be secondary to the text in Deut. 5:13-14. The texts of the Sabbath law in both Exod. 20 and Deut. 5 have suffered secondary mixing, and the reference in Deut. 5 comes from the P law in Exod. 20.

or less all the way through to Numbers 10, the last law Moses hears
from God becomes the first law he delivers to the people, a move
that points to the extreme importance the priests of the sixth century
placed upon their reinterpretation of Sabbath as a weekly instead of
monthly observance:

> Moses assembled all the congregation of the people of Israel, and
> said to them, "These are the things which Yahweh has commanded
> you to do. Six days shall work be done, but on the seventh day
> you shall have a holy Sabbath of Sabbath rest for Yahweh; whoever
> does any work on it shall be put to death; you shall kindle no fire
> in all your habitations on the Sabbath day." (Exod. 35:1-3)

The priests' status as an elite meat-eating class is reinforced by an
edict making the priests' fire the only legitimate fire on the Sabbath.
No meat may be cooked except at the priestly altar. Later in the
narrative, the injunction against kindling a fire on the Sabbath will
be stringently enforced:

> While the people of Israel were in the wilderness, they found a man
> gathering sticks [for making a fire] on the Sabbath day. And those
> who found him gathering sticks brought him to Moses and Aaron,
> and to all the congregation. They put him in custody, because it
> had not been made plain what should be done to him. Yahweh said
> to Moses, "The man shall be put to death; all the congregation shall
> stone him with stones outside the camp." All the congregation
> brought him outside the camp, and stoned him to death with stones,
> as Yahweh commanded Moses. (Num. 15:32-36, RSV, slightly
> modified)

The Sabbath law receives special sanction, since in the priestly view
it is the law that epitomizes and stands for all the laws of Moses as
revised by the Aaronid priesthood of sixth-century Judah (cf. Ezek.
20:12).

Following the Sabbath command, Moses invites contributions of
materials for constructing the tabernacle. The priestly writer's concept
that the cult of God is practiced at the tabernacle instead of the temple
is regarded by most historians as an abstraction to help conceptualize
the way in which God could be worshiped during the Babylonian
exile when the temple did not exist.[17] Following the detailed instructions concerning the tabernacle, Moses summons Bezalel and Oholiab

17. Recently some historians have suggested that even during the monarchic period the tabernacle

to begin their work. The work is carried out (Exodus 35–40), the sacrifices to be made at the tabernacle are described (Leviticus 1–7), the priests ordained (Leviticus 8–10), and the blood taboos and attending sacrifices prescribed (Leviticus 11–16).

LEVITICUS

Leviticus 16 describes the sacrifice and scapegoat for the annual day of ransom, or composition ("atonement"). Although the day of ransom falls on the tenth day of the seventh month, as defined by the moon, it is designated a Sabbath, and brings to a conclusion the long section in which the priestly writer has laid out in detail the priestly prerogative of the disposition of blood:

> It shall be a statute to you for ever that in the seventh month, on the tenth day of the month, you shall afflict yourselves, and shall do no work, either the native or the stranger who sojourns among you; for on this day shall ransom be made for you, to cleanse you; from all your sins you shall be clean before Yahweh. It is a Sabbath of Sabbath rest to you. (Lev. 16:29-31, RSV, slightly modified)

Leviticus 17–26 is the final distinctive section of laws in the priestly version of the Sinai covenant. Often referred to as the "law of holiness," it stresses that the people ought to be holy in the same way that God is holy: "You shall be holy, for I, Yahweh your God, am holy" (Leviticus 19:2). It begins with a reiteration of the priestly blood prerogatives (Leviticus 17) and the specification of incest taboos, also based on blood relationships (Leviticus 18). Then it defines the duties of the holy people. The Sabbath is placed near the beginning of these duties: "Every one of you shall revere his mother and his father, and you shall keep my Sabbaths" (Leviticus 19:3). The Sabbath law is quickly repeated: "You shall keep my Sabbaths and reverence my sanctuary" (19:30).

Toward the end of the holiness law, the priestly writer elaborates on the three great temple feasts: passover, weeks, and booths (Leviticus 23). But first, as if to stress that its status is on a par with annual festivals, the importance of the Sabbath is reiterated:

> The appointed feasts of Yahweh, the holy convocations, which you shall proclaim at the time appointed for them, are these. Six days

---

stood within the temple, so that there is no contradiction between the priestly view and the existence of the temple of the Jerusalemite priesthood. Most, however, continue to see a theoretical element in the priestly writer's conception, if only because he makes no mention of the temple whatever.

shall work be done; but on the seventh day is a Sabbath of Sabbath rest, a holy convocation; you shall do no work; it is a Sabbath to Yahweh in all your dwellings. (Lev. 23:2-3, RSV, slightly modified)

The three feasts are then described. For the priestly writer, each of the harvest feasts is to be celebrated for a Sabbath, or week, of days.

The first feast, that of the lambs and the barley harvest, is to be celebrated by killing the passover lamb and eating unleavened bread for seven days. The second, the festival of the wheat harvest, is prescribed to take place seven sets of seven days—or seven Sabbaths—after the first. It is therefore called *shabu'ot,* or "weeks" (also in English "shavuot"). In all likelihood the feast of the wheat harvest was not called "weeks" prior to the time of the priestly writer, but simply the harvest festival. The third festive period falls in the seventh month, which has the fullest set of special days, including the new year feast, the day of ransom, and the feast of booths.

Before the composition of the priestly history, the first and third feasts—the barley and fruit harvests—had been celebrated beginning on the "Sabbath" of their respective months, meaning the full moon of their lunar months. Here the priestly writer is combining two different categories—the lunar month and the Sabbath day. The month is assumed to begin with the new moon and the fifteenth to be a Sabbath, or seventh day in a recurring seven-day cycle.

In the case of the second feast, the wheat harvest, in the priestly conception the law of the covenant of Moses at Sinai was delivered at a time coincident with this harvest (Exod. 19:1). It was therefore most important to assimilate this to the weekly Sabbath pattern. If Sabbaths have been counted off regularly all along, there is only a one-in-seven chance that the fifteenth of the lunar month will fall on a Sabbath.[18] Although the inconsistency of the seventh-day and full-moon Sabbath remains in the prescription for the barley and fruit feasts in Leviticus 23, the wheat feast is brought fully within the seven-day Sabbath scheme. The wheat harvest is to be celebrated seven sets of seven days after the barley harvest. This is the origin of Pentecost, the "fiftieth" day after Passover, starting at the end of the forty-ninth.

After prescribing the baking of special bread each Sabbath (Lev. 24:5-9), the priestly writers conclude their presentation of the Sabbath

---

18. Perhaps the priestly writer means the feast to begin on the Sabbath closest to the fifteenth of the month. Or perhaps his theory is not meant to make a precise match with reality, as is the case with other aspects of the priestly revision of the temple history.

covenant with a full description of what had been the law of remission of debt in Israel. Previous tradition, described in Deuteronomy 15, held that every seventh year all debts were to be remitted—although that year was not called a Sabbath prior to the time of the priestly writers. For the priestly writers, the tradition changed. The remission of debt was assimilated to the priestly concept of Sabbath. The notion of a Sabbath of Sabbaths was extended to a redefinition of the seven-year period of debt remission and stretched to fifty years, following the pattern of the harvest of the basic staple, wheat, and its feast called by the priestly writer "weeks." Debt remission comes after counting off seven "Sabbaths" of years. The priestly writers call this year of debt remission and the restoration of land to the original owners "jubilee"[19] (Lev. 25:8-55). This climactic law is given as in some ways the most important extension of the Sabbath law.[20]

The seventh year was renamed the Sabbath and made to apply not to debt but, abstractly and artificially, to fallow.[21] Every seventh year, instead of remitting debt, people were to let their land lie fallow:

> When you come into the land which I give you, the land shall keep a Sabbath to Yahweh. Six years you shall sow your field, and six years you shall prune your vineyard, and gather its fruits; but in the seventh year there shall be a Sabbath of Sabbath rest for the land, a Sabbath to Yahweh; you shall not sow your field or prune your vineyard. What grows of itself in your harvest you shall not reap, and the grapes of your undressed vine you shall not gather; it shall be a year of Sabbath rest for the land. (Lev. 25:2-5, RSV, slightly modified)

Most historians believe that this prescription could apply only in theory, and that only a priestly class who had little if any contact with actual farming could make such a rule. A seventh-year fallow would quickly deplete the soil of Palestine, where village field systems in biblical times must have been similar to later known practice, involving fallow every two or three years. The priestly theory follows the pattern established by God's instruction not to collect manna on the seventh day. The fallow of the land seemed to the priests a fitting extension to the land of the law of periodic refraining from work.

---

19. This term originated as an approximate equivalent of the Hebrew term *yobel* and has no relation at all to Latin *jubilare* and words derived from it, like jubilation.
20. It will be discussed further in chapter 11.
21. Neh. 10:31 may imply that the Sabbath year applied then to debt also.

Some historians believe that, unlike the law of Sabbath–year fallow in Leviticus 25:2-7, the law of fallowing in Exodus 23:10-11 is archaic. It is not clear whether Exodus 23:10-11 is based on the priestly law or does in fact predate the priestly history. In either case, the priestly statement of the sabbatical fallow is abstracted from farming practice. What this practice was is unknown, but it is possible that "each farmer left a seventh of his land fallow each year, thus providing rest for the land and food for the poor."[22] Alternatively, a biennial fallowing system may have been applied to a farmer's holdings divided into two parts: "The sabbatical year would break the normal rotation for only that half of the farmer's holdings which were scheduled to be cropped in that year."[23] This loss could be compensated for by cropping both parts in the year prior to the sabbatical. Of course, the priestly law is more rigid and makes no allowance for divided holdings. The idealized seven-year cycle of fallowing is reminiscent of the priest Ezekiel's conception of the land tenure of the twelve tribes of Israel, whose holdings are made "equal" merely by making them of equal north-south dimensions, disregarding the differences in terrain and soil in the east-west dimension (Ezekiel 48).[24]

This section of laws is followed by a conclusion in which blessings are promised for obedience to the covenant and curses threatened for disobedience (Leviticus 26). Israel's survival and autonomy is linked to obedience to the whole of the law, but especially to observance of the Sabbath:

> You shall keep my Sabbaths and reverence my sanctuary: I am the Lord (Lev. 26:2)

If Israelites did not keep the Sabbath and the Aaronid revision of the Mosaic laws which this day stood for, they would be deported from their land, their cities laid waste:

> Then the land shall enjoy its Sabbaths as long as it lies desolate, while you are in your enemies' land; then the land shall rest, and enjoy its Sabbaths. As long as it lies desolate it shall have rest, the rest which it had not in your Sabbaths when you dwelt upon it. (Lev. 26:34-35, RSV)

22. Oded Borowski, *Agriculture in Iron Age Israel* (Winona Lake: Eisenbrauns, 1987), 145.
23. David C. Hopkins, *The Highlands of Canaan: Agricultural Life in the Early Iron Age* (Decatur: Almond Press, 1985), 194–95, 200-202, 273.
24. Nevertheless, references in I Maccabees 6:49, 53 to keeping the Sabbath year are often cited as indicating the law was in fact in effect in the later biblical period.

9

A World Centered in a Tent

Creation in ancient texts means creation of the state and its social order. At the heart of the state and its ordered way of life sit the temple and its cult. The temple is the prime focus of law and order in the state, and therefore the pinnacle of creation.

THE TABERNACLE

It comes as no surprise that the focus of the priestly revision of the official temple history of Israel is on the tabernacle. The tabernacle is an elaborate tent where God encounters the people and receives their offerings, especially of meat. It is the place where divine order is infused into the cosmos.

Nor does it come as a surprise that the tabernacle is created by the same spirit or breath that hovered over the water in Genesis 1. This "breath of God" (RSV: "Spirit of God") is mentioned in only two other places in the whole of the priestly history. Even as creation commenced as the "breath of God was moving over the face of the water" (Gen. 1:2), so also this spirit inspired the craftsman who supervised the building of the tabernacle:

> See, I have called by name Bezalel the son of Uri, son of Hur, of the tribe of Judah. I have filled him with the breath of God, with ability and intelligence, with knowledge and all craftsmanship. (Exod. 31:2-3, RSV, altered)

Bezalel's job is to direct the construction of the tabernacle. He gains the capacity to perform this momentous service by the same breath of God that was manifest at the scene of creation and that was active as God breathed out, one after another, his creative commands:

> Yahweh has called by name Bezalel the son of Uri, son of Hur, of the tribe of Judah, and has filled him with the breath of God, with ability, with intelligence, with knowledge, and with all craftsmanship. (Exod. 35:30-31)

This creative and skillful breath of God is described in Job: "It is the breath in a person, the breath of Shadday, that gives a person understanding" (32:8). "The breath of God has made me, and the breath of Shadday gives me life" (33:4). The meaning of Hebrew *ruaḥ* is ambiguous. It can mean wind, spirit, or breath. That it means breath here is made clear by its being teamed with a second word that means only breath, and by the mention of the same skillful understanding that inspires Bezalel. It is also noteworthy that the Job passages mention Shadday, the distinctive name of God in the priestly age of Abraham beginning in Genesis 17.

Bezalel's inspired attributes, skill, understanding, and knowledge, are identical to those of the craftsman Hiram who worked on the first Jerusalem temple (Exod. 31:3; 1 Kings 7:14). The breath of God that gave him these attributes was regarded as essential to the process of the reconstruction of the temple in the time of the Aaronid priestly writers. The prophet Haggai proclaimed in God's name the conditions of the restoration of the priestly cult in these terms: "Take courage, Zerubbabel, take courage, Joshua, the son of Jehozadak, the high priest, and take courage, all people of the land; work [on the temple], for I am with you, according to the promise I made you when you came out of Egypt: my breath abides in your midst; fear not" (Hag. 2:4-5).

The instructions for the construction of the tabernacle, its furniture, and the vestments of the priesthood are divided into seven speeches (Exodus 25–31). The speeches, each beginning with "Yahweh said to Moses," appear to parallel the seven days of creation, with one for each day of creation.[1] The last speech on the seventh day appropriately concerns the Sabbath as the sign of the climactic eternal covenant.

---

1. Some of the allusions to creation in the remaining six speeches are clearer than others, but the principle does seem to make sense of the order of instructions. See Peter J. Kearney, "Creation and Liturgy: The P Redaction of Ex 25–40," *Zeitschrift für die alttestamentliche Wissenschaft* 89 (1977): 375–87.

The first speech is the longest and has two parts. The first part uses the term "tabernacle" (*mishkan*), and the second the term "tent of meeting" (ɔ*ohel moᶜed*), for the sanctuary.

> "Tent of Meeting" is an apt name in this second section, where the redactor builds climactically towards a continuous sequence of cultic "meetings" with God (29:38-43). The divine establishing of the Aaronid priesthood is a proximate preparation for these "meetings" and, most significantly, at the beginning and within the conclusion of this second part, there is mentioned Aaron's care of the lamps (27:20-21, 30:7-8).[2]

Just as God brought light into darkness, so Aaron caused light to shine in the shrine's interior and the night. Each of the succeeding speeches makes a similar allusion to creation. For example, the third speech concerns the fashioning of the bronze laver or basin (30:17-21). "The association between this object and the third day of creation, when God created *yammim*, 'seas,' is made obvious through 1 Kings 7:23, where the bronze laver is called *hayyam*, 'the sea.' "[3]

The account of the building of the tabernacle has also been shown to follow the pattern of the account of the building of the temple in 1 Kings 5:15—9:25, which itself is patterned like other accounts from Mesopotamia and Ugarit. This pattern includes the elements of divine command, the passing on of the command to the people, preparations for building the sanctuary, the actual construction, the dedication, and the blessing.[4]

YAHWEH AS EL

Since the tabernacle stands at the heart of the state and is the primary means of enforcing law and order, we might expect it to have military connotations. There can be little doubt that the tabernacle as thought of by the Aaronid author of the priestly history was modeled after the tent of El, one of the pre-Israelite gods many of whose attributes were also seen in the God of Israel.[5] El was a warrior god, like a

---

2. Ibid., 375.
3. Ibid., 377.
4. Victor (Avigdor) Hurowitz, "The Priestly Account of Building the Tabernacle," *Journal of the American Oriental Society* 105 (1985): 21–30.
5. See especially Frank M. Cross, Jr., "The Tabernacle: A Study from an Archaeological and Historical Approach," *Biblical Archaeologist* 10 (1947): 45–68; reprinted in *The Biblical Archaeologist Reader,* ed. G. Ernest Wright and David Noel Freedman (Garden City: Doubleday, 1961), 201–28. See also Cross, "The Priestly Tabernacle in the Light of Recent Research," in *The Temple in Antiquity,* ed. T. G. Madsden (Provo: Religious Studies Center, Brigham Young University, 1984), 91–105.

paramilitary bedouin chieftain. The priestly writer pictures Israel in
military formation departing from Egypt, and El is seen leading his
military host through the wilderness as it marches and encamps during
the desert trek. The tabernacle, including its ark throne, functioned
historically as a battle palladium, and this is the way it is portrayed
in the priestly history.

The name of the chief craftsman of God's tabernacle, Bezalel, is a
strange name in English, but in Hebrew it is made up of a meaningful
phrase, like many Hebrew names. The name is significant for the
tabernacle that its bearer is to construct. The element *zal* means
"shade" or "shelter," and Bezalel means "in-the-shelter-of-El." The
"El" at the end of Bezalel is the same El who was the warrior god.
El also refers to Israel's God in the name El Shadday, a name for God
used uniquely by the priestly writer.

El was a patriarchal sheikh among the gods. His authoritative word,
like the word of God in Genesis 1, was particularly potent. And, as
demonstrated by certain Ugaritic texts known since the 1930s, El
lived in a tent, in contrast to the house, or temple, built for Baal.
Before his victory over Sea, Baal lived with El: "Baal has no house
like the other gods, no court like Asherah's sons; El's abode is his
son's [Baal's] shelter, Lady Asherah-of-the-Sea's abode."[6] The word
"shelter" that here describes El's tent is a form of the same word as
"shelter" in Bezalel's name: "in-the-*shelter*-of-El."

The same word occurs in a description of the cultic shrine built by
the Ugaritic hero Kirta. Kirta's shrine is to El, so it is fittingly a tent,
though it is talked about as though it had houselike attributes as well:

> Kirta looked, and it was a dream;
> El's servant had had a vision.
> He washed himself and applied red ointment,
> he washed his arm to the elbow,
> from his fingers to his shoulder.
> He entered *the shelter of the tent.*
> He took a lamb in his hand,
> a sacrificial lamb in his right hand,
> a young animal in both his hands,
> all the food which accompanies the libation.
> He took the proper sacrificial bird,

6. Coogan, *Stories from Ancient Canaan* (Philadelphia: Westminster Press, 1978), 96–97.

> he poured wine from a silver goblet,
> honey from a golden bowl,
> and he went up to the top of the tower,
> he climbed to the height of the wall;
> he raised his hands to heaven,
> he sacrificed to the Bull, his father El. . . .[7]

Kirta's tent shrine of sacrifice to El is in these features an exact replica of the priestly tabernacle.

A further, somewhat obscure, expression in Ugaritic may also figure in the picture of God in the priestly history. El in the Ugaritic texts is said to have a *dh-d* (these are only the consonants of the word; the vowels are not represented in Ugaritic writing). Some historians equate this *dh-d* with Ugaritic *th-d*. The meaning of *th-d* and *dh-d* would be "mountain or dome," referring to the dome of a tent. This term would appear in Hebrew with the sound *sh* instead of *th*, hence *shad(d)*, or, with the suffix *-ay, shadday*.[8] The name *Shadday-àmmi* occurs in an Egyptian inscription from the fourteenth or early thirteenth century B.C.E.[9] It is the name of someone from Palestine who resides in Egypt. The priestly writer is using an archaic name element, as he so often does in his history. It is probable that El Shadday in the priestly history meant "El the Tenting One" (or "El the Mountain One"). The tent is the same tent referred to in Bezalel's name, the tent of El that is the model for the priestly tabernacle.[10]

WHY A TENT?

The Aaronid priests were the successors of priestly families of the temple of the house of David prior to the temple's destruction by the Babylonians. The ritual traditions contained in the priestly history pertained to the temple. Why, then, does the priestly writer picture the priestly shrine as a tent rather than a temple?

It is possible that the archaic tent shrine of the time of David and before continued to be set up inside the temple during the monarchic

---

7. Ibid., 59, 62.
8. Frank M. Cross, *Canaanite Myth and Hebrew Epic* (Cambridge: Harvard University Press, 1973), 55, n. 43.
9. See William Foxwell Albright, *From the Stone Age to Christianity*, 2d ed. (Garden City: Doubleday, 1957), 243–46.
10. The meaning of *Shadday* as a name of God has long been the subject of dispute among historians. The traditional translation "God Almighty" is based on the early Greek translation, which was more or less arbitrary. The name *Silletay* held by two persons in the Old Testament probably means "he of the tent shrine."

period, and that this arrangement is one reason the priestly writer speaks of the cult shrine as a tent.[11] However, it is significant that there is no mention whatever of the temple in the priestly work. Even if the tent shrine stood in the temple, there are other reasons that the priests of the sixth century conceived of the cult as a tent cult.

The priests were archaizers, and the idea that God was to be worshiped in a tent was one more example of this archaizing impulse. The postulated tent shrines of early Israel were not replaced by the temple until the time of Solomon. The memory of a tent shrine of the time of David and before, apparently found in the Bible's earliest history, is preserved in the priestly writer's conception of the period of Moses and the exodus. This is clear from his designation of the tabernacle as a *mishkan*, a term that meant "tent" in the earlier biblical period and that had an associated derived verb meaning "to tent." These words may have been little used in the priestly cult during the monarchic period, but were picked up again by the priestly writer during the exile to refer exclusively to the priestly tabernacle.[12] Was it also possible that the priestly writer understood, at least in some implicit way, that the Israelite God Yahweh was in reality a form of the pre-Israelite god El, who lived in a tent rather than a temple?

The priestly history was a revision of the earlier temple history of Israel (JE) as it was known to the expatriate priests of the court of the house of David during the period of the Babylonian exile in the mid-sixth century B.C.E. They tried where possible to accommodate their conceptions to the conceptions of this document. The original history, written prior to the building of Solomon's temple, knows only a tent shrine of God, with a modest fieldstone altar for sacrifice. The tent shrine was a given in the document the priestly writer set out to revise. He does not alter this tradition but elaborates it into the priestly tabernacle.

There was also a practical reason for describing a tent cult. The temple had been destroyed. Its sacrificial rite as practiced during the times of the kings of Judah had ceased. Where was the temple's God located amid this utter disruption? God was not resident at the temple, whose cult had ceased to exist, and it was uncertain whether he ever would be again. The conception of a movable God—a God who could

---

11. Richard E. Friedman, *Who Wrote the Bible?* (New York: Summit Books, 1987), 174–87. It remains to be seen whether historians will find this interesting view convincing.
12. Cross, "The Priestly Tabernacle," 224–26.

travel over the world to be present with Judahites wherever they might be—had already been presented in Ezekiel's vision of God departing from the temple in a wheeled chariot capable of going off in all four directions (Ezek. 1, 10, 11:22-25). The God of the tent shrine had a contingency that fit the priestly experience of the communal sin that had brought on the destruction of the temple, and a movability that accorded with the hope and expectation that the cult of God could somehow be reconstituted. In a word, the veneration of the tabernacle was a fall-back position in the face of the loss of the temple. Indeed, the Aaronids may have conducted their cult at a tent prior to the rebuilding of the temple in approximately 520–515 B.C.E.

TENT OF "MEETING"

Whether in exile or in the land of Palestine, the tabernacle was the location where God came to meet with his people Israel. Hence it was called *ɔohel moꜥed*, which the priestly writer took to mean "*tent* of the *meeting* between God and his people." But this was not the original meaning of the term. In early Hebrew and related languages, and in certain passages in the Bible as well, the term *moꜥed* meant "assembly" in general. For example, it appears in an eleventh-century B.C.E. Egyptian text as a loanword from Phoenician, closely related to Hebrew, referring to the city assembly of Byblos in deliberation. The tent of El, therefore, was originally the "tent of assembly," where the patriarchal sheikh El held counsel with his fellow nobles and chiefs. The priestly writer, while faithfully preserving the archaic term, understands it differently. He regards several words having the consonants ꜥ and *d* to be related to one another, and takes *moꜥed* to be one of them:

> The central purpose of ritual, in [P's] view, is that of *meeting* with God, expressed in various related Hebrew words: *noꜥad* (verbal form), "to meet, encounter"; *moꜥed* (nominal form), "meeting, appointed time"; and another nominal form, *ꜥedah*, "congregation." Israel is an *ꜥedah*, a "congregation," and the tent-shrine is the "tent of meeting" (*moꜥed*). There Yahweh "meets" (*noꜥad*) with the Israelites. Speaking of the use of the sacred trumpets, the priestly writer uses all three: "And when they blow them, all the congregation [*ꜥedah*] shall assemble [*noꜥedu*] before you at the entrance to the tent of meeting [*moꜥed*]" (Numbers 10:3). From this solid pier of terminology P erects a bridge to the covenant idea. *ꜥedut*, his

word for the Sinai pact, with its combination of the consonants ʿ
and *d* (ʿ*ayin* and *daleth*), sounds a lot like his "meeting" words, as
though they were all derived from the same base. This is not so
. . . but it permits a barrage of assonance that leaves the impression
that "covenant" and "meeting" really are much the same. So the
tabernacle is interchangeably "tent of ʿ*edut*" and "tent of *moʿed*,"
and P likes to combine the elements in sentences: "You shall put
some of it [incense] in front of the pact [ʿ*edut*] in the tent of meeting
[*moʿed*], where I will meet ['*iwwaʿed*] with you." (Exodus 30:36;
compare 30:6; Numbers 17:19)[13]

The climactic description of God's meeting with Israel at the tent
of meeting comes just after the initial prescriptions for the tent and
priesthood. Here also these terms appear in combination:

> It shall be a continual burnt offering throughout your generations
> at the door of the tent of meeting before Yahweh, where I will
> meet with you, to speak there to you. There I will meet with the
> people of Israel, and it shall be sanctified by my glory; I will con-
> secrate the tent of meeting and the altar; Aaron also and his sons I
> will consecrate, to serve me as priests. And I will tent [*shkn*] among
> the people of Israel, and will be their God. (Exod. 29:42-45, RSV)[14]

YAHWEH'S *KABOD*

In what form does God meet with his people, in this tent cult that is
the focal point of creation, the implied core of the created order? In
the priestly history, God characteristically meets with his people in
the form of his "glory." What is this glory, or *kabod*?

The translation of *kabod* as "glory" comes from the Greek translation of the original Hebrew text and, like "God Almighty" (which
is how El Shadday is translated by the Greek), represents something
of a guess. The term *kabod* is a technical priestly term. In the priestly
history, Ezekiel, and Second and Third Isaiah (Isaiah 40–66), it is the
usual term for the manifestation of the presence of God. Its ordinary
meaning is "weightiness," or something that is "weighty." The priestly

---

13. Delbert R. Hillers, *Covenant: The History of a Biblical Idea* (Baltimore: Johns Hopkins University
Press, 1969), 163–64. There remains uncertainty whether ʿ*edut* originally meant "treaty stipulation"
or "testimony, instruction"; see B. Couroyer, "ʿEDUT: Stipulation de traité ou enseignement?"
Revue biblique 95 (1988): 321–31.
14. "Underlying the massive detail of the Priestly strata is one dominant theme . . . : under the
conditions of the desert covenant, Yahweh will 'tabernacle' in the midst of his people Israel (Exod.
25:8; 29:45,46; 40:35; and often: cf. Lev. 26:11)" Cross, "The Priestly Tabernacle," 225.

usage has two related aspects based on the root connotation of weight-iness. One is honor, a frequent meaning of *kabod*. In the priestly history, the honor of God is seen in the control that God manifests over creation and its orders. If there were any doubt about the power and dignity of God, it is immediately dispelled by the spectacle of God delivering a series of fiats that are instantly obeyed. This portrayal of God's control over creation offsets the feeling of loss of control experienced by the priests in their Babylonian exile. God's presence at the tent manifests the honor of Israel's God in the face of the dishonor of the destruction of the temple and its cult. That dishonor is not the last word. God's *kabod* confers a dignity on the new priestly cult that counteracts the indignity of the disenfranchisement of the priestly families, who, like God, are to exercise dominion over creation:

> Then God said, "Let us make humanity in our image, after our likeness; and let them have dominion over the fish of the sea, and over the birds of the air, and over the cattle, and over all the earth, and over every creeping thing that creeps upon the earth." So God created humanity in his own image, in the image of God he created them; male and female he created them. And God blessed them, and God said to them, "Be fruitful and multiply, and fill the earth and subdue it; and have dominion over the fish of the sea and over the birds of the air and over every living thing that moves upon the earth." (Gen. 1:26-28, RSV, slightly modified)

The idea that God was present to his people in his *kabod* did not originate with the priests of the court of Jehoiachin and his successors in exile. It went back long before then. God's honor and the dignity of the priestly cult had always been priestly concerns, though they were brought to the fore with particular poignancy by the circum-stances of the sixth century.

Another meaning just as basic to the priestly understanding of the presence of God perhaps more clearly represents a tradition going back deep into the monarchic period and even earlier. The term *kabod* was applied to the heavy dark cloud of smoke that persisted contin-uously over the altar of the sacrificial cult, whether of the temple or tabernacle. This cloud, perceived as "weighty," or "heavy," hovered over the altar and tabernacle much as the breath of God hovered over the waters at the beginning of creation.

This cloud of smoke was also regarded as analogous with the storm cloud of the victorious warrior God. God rode the clouds like a divine

chariot, descending to earth to achieve victory and ascending to heaven
to retake his throne. This traditional military connotation of the *kabod*
conforms to the military conception of the people of God in the priestly
history. The cloud was typically luminescent as well, from the flash
and lightning in the storm cloud and the flame of fire and sparks
springing from the altar. The Greek translation of *kabod* as "glory"
captures the numinous luminescence of the pillars of cloud and fire
of the exodus, which are merged in the priestly conception.

The cloud of smoke ascends from the altar fire. The chief activity
of the cult of the tent was the offering of meat by burning or cooking
on the altar. The altar sacrifice was the heart of the priestly cult, the
focal point of Israel's relation to God, and, through Israel, the focal
point of the whole of humanity's relation to God.

In the priestly writer's grandiose presumption, following the tradition of the original author of the official temple history in the time
of David, and ratified by others such as the inspiring Second Isaiah
(Isaiah 40–55), the cult of Jerusalem represents nothing less than the
center of the world created in the priestly account of creation. Such
presumption is an old and common story. Most social groups have
the tendency to regard themselves as occupying the center of the
world. The Aaronid priests of the late sixth century B.C.E. were not
unique in this regard.

10

The Opulent and
the Messy

The centerpiece of the priestly rite that lies at the heart of the priestly history, including the account of creation in Genesis 1, is the sacrifice of meat by fire. This sacrificial rite is central even to those texts in which it is neither mentioned nor alluded to.

MEAT AND BLOOD

At its most lavish, the work of the leading priests in Palestine during the biblical period was a singular mixture of the opulent and the messy. The priests clothed themselves in expensive white linen girdles, cloaks, and caps, tailored from fine imported linen. Other cloth in which they were dressed was dyed gold, blue, purple, and scarlet. Gold filigree twined on the garments. The priestly stole was covered with inlaid precious stones of great variety, some of them skillfully engraved. The priests worked with vessels and instruments made of bronze and lined and framed with gold. The installation of the priests was accomplished with costly scented olive oil. About the priestly workplace hovered the odors of incense imported from distant places at great effort and expense. It is likely that incense was not readily available even in elite circles prior to the time of the priestly writing.

All about was the bleating, braying, cackling, clucking, barking, and howling of the animals, sacrificial and otherwise. The smells of manure, blood, and burning and roasting flesh alternately filled the air. Patient attendants led, dragged, and carted the animals about, kept the fires going, cleared away ashes, offal, and other refuse, and brushed away unwanted dogs and birds. The area was thick with flies. Some priests had finished consuming their daily meat dinner, others were waiting their turn, hungry to enjoy some residue of their effort. The grain bins and honey and incense pots contributed their smells to the scene. Outside the precinct, acceptable animals had to be bartered for, prayers said, songs sung, and accompanying family and friends cared for. Such was the sacrificial cult of the Jerusalem temple.

It is necessary to bear in mind that the daily service of the priests was an extremely bloody affair. The priests would slaughter the beast, controlling the flow of blood as well as possible. Then the priest with his fingers would spread blood on the altar, and during ordination on the ears, thumbs, and toes of other priests. After this, he would pour blood at the base of the altar, and sometimes all about the altar. Then the carcass was butchered and parts burned on the altar or transported beyond the sanctuary precinct for burning. With all these procedures carried out, it is difficult to imagine the priest was able to keep his linen cloak and cap perfectly clean. On the contrary, there would be blood all over the place, spattered here, splashed there, smeared everywhere. The ritual for cleansing after recovery from spotted disease involved a magical antispotting, which consisted of dipping a leafy hyssop branch in blood and shaking it to sprinkle blood spots on the affected item.

Even a quick reading of Exodus 29, the prescription for the ordination of priests, will convey a vivid impression of the prevalence in the cult of channeled, sprinkled, and smeared blood. There is evidence, furthermore, that the priests of Israel were not alone in regarding blood as an element of life in the living being.

Priestly sacrifice by fire is somewhat of a misnomer in more ways than one. The use of fire was limited, and the priests were not the ones who were really making a sacrifice. In fact, much of what was brought to the altar at the temple or tabernacle was put to practical use as food for the priests. With the exception of the so-called peace offering, which reverted to the donor, sacrifice was not a forfeiture on the part of the beast's butcher or cereal's scorcher, but an act of forfeiture on the part of the donor. Not only was there no loss for the priest, there was a gain.

Just a small portion of one menu for temple priests' portions of meat from Mesopotamia runs as follows:[1]

1. Gilbert J. P. McEwan, "Distribution of Meat in Eanna," *Iraq* 45 (1983): 187-98, esp. p. 192.

25. (The second) regular offering sheep
    before Istar of Uruk and Nana, which
    (is butchered) daily:

26. A shoulder, the rump and a rib roast—	rations of the king
27. The heart, a kidney, the *nasrapu* and a choice shoulder cut—	the chief priest
28. A shoulder, a rib roast, the breast and the spleen—	the priests
29. A choice shoulder cut, a kidney and the spleen—	the priests
30. A leg and the back—	the king
31. (One half of the other) leg—	the chief administrator
32. (One half of the other) leg—	the priests
33. The penis (?) and testicles (?)—	the *bit hilsu*
34. ("The gate")—	the chariot priest
35. (The neck)—	the *kalu*-priest
36. (The head)—	the singer
37. (The . . . of the ribs)—	the *zabardabbu*
38. (The reticulum)—	(the brewer)
39. (The . . . and the) omasum—	(the baker)
40. (One half of the) hide—	(the king)
41. (One half of the) hide—	(the priests)

The list goes on for scores of lines and reads like a butcher's department at a supermarket.

SACRIFICE AND SOCIAL ORDER

Considering that the priests fared so well from the people's sacrifices, what induced the populace to donate so lavishly their valuable livestock and crops to the official cult and its practitioners, especially when the populace themselves had little if any interest in the intricacies of the priestly blood taboos?

There is no evidence to suggest that priestly troops compelled or extorted such donations, or that social pressure forced compliance. People brought their offerings because they believed the temple to be the locus of God's presence, and therefore the place of divine blessing or cursing. The rationales offered by the elite temple priests for their costly sacrifical rites reinforced this popular notion.

The priests theorized that the world was imbued with a pervasive and abiding order determined at its creation. This created order was the inherent norm in terms of which every form of disorder—all the instability, insecurity, arbitrariness, and deviation experienced in the real world—was to be addressed and managed. In the fateful, capricious world of ancient Palestine, most considered they had no choice but to believe that through such cults an individual could indeed make contact with the divine, and perhaps sway the gods and chance in their favor, or at least ward off their devastating and unpredictable wrath.

In the judgment of the priests, the epitome of disorder was loose blood, arguably the most conspicuous manifestation of the loss of life, which loss was surely itself near the top of the list of people's experiences of disorder. The priestly cult offered to govern loose blood, to restore the flow of blood to its prescribed place in the framework of the created order, and in so doing to signify also the resolution of other social experiences of disorder, through sacrifices specified for such purposes as purgation, pacification, compensation, and reparation. The motif that underlies the entire roster of sacrifices is thus the restoration of the order created by God, as revealed in the priestly cult.

At the heart of the issue of order was the concern for social order. The priestly cults of Palestine presumed to embody divine concern for social order. Such a boon was worth respecting, if not actively supporting. At the least, it was prudent to avoid giving offense to such cults. If the appeal of sacrifice was to salvage God's order, what better cause to which to contribute a male beast? Who would fail to donate to a procedure that promised donors themselves, life's unwilling prey, the opportunity to contribute to the restitution of social order?

The service of the cult paralleled the service of a sovereign lord and his court, and the social experience of relating to such a court. Most Judahites in the time of the priestly writers had nothing to do with such courts if they could help it. When they were forced to do so, they normally related to them only through their patrons, who functioned as intermediaries on behalf of peasant clients. The same held for the cult of sacrifice in the provincial capital Jerusalem in the sixth century B.C.E. (as it did in the monarchic period also). In effect, the Aaronid priesthood served as intermediaries for the "community" of Judah in the court of God, symbolized by the tabernacle, which stood for the tent of El's assembly.

Most if not all of the reasons people sacrificed in ancient societies can be recognized in the priestly text of the Jerusalem temple, if not explicitly then implicitly. Neither Palestinian practice nor the practice outlined in the Hebrew scriptures was distinctive.[2] Sacrifices were made as propitiatory gifts to secure some favor from God. They were made as tribute to God in recognition of God's sovereign grace in providing produce and livestock for people's use. They were made pursuant to a vow or promise to pay God in return for a favor requested—such sacrifices are called votive. They were made as an expression of simple thanks for a particular blessing. The scriptures also make mention of voluntary, or freewill, sacrifices, made apparently on impulse and hence falling on the periphery of the usual complex priestly procedures.

In addition to the sacrifice as gift, sacrifices were made, in theory, to feed God. Texts like Psalm 50 which strain to deny this purpose show that it was a common conception. In the cult described by the priestly writers, meat or grain burned on the altar was regarded as food for God. With any meat sacrifice, all blood and discrete fat deposits belonged to God. Some sacrifices involved a meal shared among God, priests, and laity.

Other sacrifices were expiatory. This is a particularly significant theoretical category in the tradition of the exiled priests, who wanted to comprehend the pervasiveness of sin corresponding to the extreme punishment of the loss of the temple's cult. Yet such expiation only represents the priests' enduring preoccupation with the restoration of order.

Much of the terminology of sacrifice in the priestly tradition is drawn from everyday spheres of life where particular words have meanings that are not specifically sacrificial. Thus the connection with the mundane is never distant. A cereal offering is called a *minḥah,* whose everyday meaning is a tribute, among other things. The "sacrifice of peace offering" (RSV) uses the term *zebaḥ,* "sacrifice," an everyday word for slaughter, or a meal involving meat. The verb translated with various forms of the English word "atone" comes

---

2. Despite attempts to present them as such. See Theodor H. Gaster, "Sacrifices," *IDBSupp,* 148–53; M. F. C. Bourdillon and Meyer Fortes, ed., *Sacrifice* (New York: Academic Press, 1980); Nancy Jay, "Sacrifice as Remedy for Having Been Born of Woman," in *Immaculate and Powerful: The Female in Sacred Image and Social Reality,* ed. Clarissa W. Atkinson, Constance H. Buchanan, and Margaret R. Miles (Boston: Beacon Press, 1985) 283–309.

from the everyday Hebrew word for "composition" in the legal sense, a payment or act for settling differences or righting some legal imbalance.[3] The term usually rendered "guilt offering" appears in nonsacrificial contexts and also refers to guilt that requires some form of indemnification.

FIVE KINDS OF SACRIFICE

The priestly text concerning sacrifice—found primarily in Leviticus 1–7—may be classed as a prescriptive ritual text, a common genre in the ancient world. This text or something like it was used in the cult as a reference document. The text is both practical and theoretical: it explains not only the main ingredients and procedures of the cult, but also its main meanings.

The offerings described in the priestly prescriptive ritual in Leviticus fall into five categories. For the first three, the main emphasis is on what the sacrifice consists of.

The first sacrifice is the whole burnt offering of meat (Leviticus 1), which can be a male head of cattle, a male lamb or kid, or a dove or pigeon. (The requirement for male animals mirrors the dominance of male humans in the cult, though ironically the purpose is to preserve female animals, which were more valuable than males for producing more animals.) The offerer slaughtered the beast, the priest disposed of its blood by collecting it and splashing it around the base of the altar, and the animal was then burnt in its entirety.

The second sacrifice is the grain offering (Leviticus 2). This could be presented in the form of flour, or of baked unleavened wafers or pieces. These were mixed with oil and topped with frankincense, an exotic spice acquired in the Arabian spice trade. The priest dipped his hand into the portion with incense and burned a fistful, including all the costly but unpalatable incense, on the altar. The rest went to balance the diet of the priest and his cohorts.

The third sacrifice, the feast of *shelem,* usually rendered "peace" or "communal" offering (Leviticus 3), was treated initially the same way as the whole burnt offering. Rather than burning the whole beast, however, the priest removed the prescribed fat parts and incinerated these for God, then turned the rest of the meat over to the offerer

3. Herbert Chanan Brichto, "On Slaughter and Sacrifice, Blood and Atonement," *Hebrew Union College Annual* 47 (1976): 19–55.

for the use of him and his family. Even in the case of this sacrifice, a transaction with God is implied in the name, which connotes a balancing, rectification, or pacification.

The fourth and fifth sacrifices were two distinct forms related specifically to wrongdoing. These were the purification or purgation offering (Lev. 4:1—5:13; RSV: "sin offering") and the penalty or reparation offering (Lev. 5:14—6:7; RSV: "guilt offering"). Both offerings were made in the event of "sin"—that is, the infringement of a taboo or the violation of a prescribed cultic or social law, in which the donor himself is in violation of God's order. Sin caused an impairment in the form of a theoretical contagion, or impurity—a sort of symptom of disorder—that attached to persons and things and had to be ritually counteracted. In other words, some "dirt" had to be "cleaned." This was done through the blood of the purification sacrifice.[4] Purification for sin, which near the beginning of the priestly history was epitomized by the shedding of blood by Cain and Lemek, involved an ironic, or magical, remedy in the form of the shedding of blood in sacrifice.

The priestly preoccupation with governing the disposition of blood is set out in Leviticus 17, immediately after the full exposition of the sacrifices of the cult, culminating with the purification sacrifice of the scapegoat. The purification sacrifice was performed with any of the previously prescribed animals except a male sheep or ram, while the penalty offering required a ram. (Though few rams were raised to maturity, a ram was by no means the most valuable animal in the flock; it may, however, have borne the most distinction in a male-dominated cult.)

With the purification sacrifice, the kind of animal was less important than the disposition of the blood. What was done with the blood of the sacrifice depended on the social position of the offerer. For the priest himself, or a body of elders representing the whole community, the blood was collected and sprinkled before the veil fronting the holiest section of the tabernacle precinct, then smeared on the horns of the altar, and poured out at the base of the altar. For a local chief (RSV "ruler") or commoner, the sprinkling of blood before the veil was omitted. Once again the priests took the opportunity to distinguish themselves from the rest of humanity.

---

4. See Dennis J. McCarthy, "The Symbolism of Blood and Sacrifice," *Journal of Biblical Literature* 88 (1969): 166–76; "Further Notes on the Symbolism of Blood and Sacrifice," *Journal of Biblical Literature* 92 (1973): 205–10.

The primary objects of purification were the sanctuary and its practitioners, as well as the donor.[5] Sin was thought to make God's sanctuary unclean, and a holy God could not dwell amid uncleanness. In order for God to be present among his people, the sanctuary had to be purified.[6] This purging was accomplished with the blood from the purification offering, which acted as a "ritual detergent."[7]

The priestly covenantal stipulations applied to all members of the community by virtue of an implied oath. "The law," in the words of one recent study, "was transmitted as an oath which was binding upon future generations, with the curses [Leviticus 26] inherent within the oath."[8] This makes the violation of the taboos and laws of the priestly covenants similar to the violation of an oath. Because there are aspects of the covenants that a person might violate, even unwittingly, some precaution is in order to annul the curse resulting from the violated oath. The purification offering covers this contingency, as described in Leviticus 5:1-6. This section refers to a person who becomes conscious of a specific wrongdoing. This consciousness may spring from the conscience, or it could be the result of a person being compelled by sickness, injury, or misfortune—brought on by the working of the curse—to search the memory for some misdeed that might have been committed. The theory comes close to a presumption of guilt until the purification rite has been rendered.

A wrongdoing resulted in more than the release of a contagion or impurity requiring purgation. There was often an identifiable social liability. In cases of theft, false oath, and deception, mentioned in Leviticus 6:1-3, it was frequently possible for the guilty party to make indemnification or reparation. The indemnification usually entailed the property at issue plus twenty percent. The guilty party might feel, or be made to feel, a further "debt to society,"[9] in which case he would make a penalty sacrifice, the second kind of offering attached to a wrongdoing. This offering was not the indemnification itself; it was

5. Noam Zohar, "Repentance and Purification: The Significance and Semantics of ḥṭ't in the Pentateuch," *Journal of Biblical Literature* 107 (1988): 609–18. The position of the donor is still disputed; note Jacob Milgrom, "The *Modus Operandi* of the ḥaṭṭaʾt: A Rejoinder," *Journal of Biblical Literature* 109 (1990): 111–17.
6. Gordon J. Wenham, *The Book of Leviticus* (The New International Commentary on the Old Testament, 3) (Grand Rapids: Eerdmans, 1979), 89.
7. Jacob Milgrom, "Sacrifices and offerings, OT," *IDBSupp*, 766.
8. M. J. Geller, "The *Šurpu* Incantations and Lev. V.1–5," *Journal of Semitic Studies* 25 (1980): 181–92. The quote is on p. 187.
9. To use Gaster's phrase.

not compensatory, but punitive. It served as a penalty payment above and beyond the indemnification itself. It was an offering that accompanied restitution, rather than serving as restitution. With the penalty sacrifice, legal "composition"—the righting, or settling, of a legal imbalance—was achieved by throwing the blood of the sacrificial ram against the altar.

One further distinction played a significant role in the priestly presentation of the purification and penalty offerings. This was the distinction between inadvertent and known misdeeds.[10] For the latter, a confession was expected, either in words or in the form of a restitution that implied a confession. "A basic postulate of the Priestly Code was that a voluntary confession reduces deliberate sins to inadvertencies, thereby rendering them eligible for sacrificial expiation."[11]

Other sacrifices in the priestly text, like the purification rites for skin disease or the scapegoat rite described in Leviticus 16, fall into one of the five main types.

OTHER OFFERINGS AND TAXES

The account of creation in Genesis 1 provided the theoretical basis for managing law and order, misdeed and reparation, through a cult whose highlight was elite consumption of meat. Sacrifice represented an attitude of tribute toward the cult as well as toward God, and an investment in the cult to maintain its place as the guarantor of law and order in the Judahite society of the Persian period. The priests received continuous provision of grain, and especially meat, to supplement the ample provisions available to them by virtue of their positions among the chief landowners of the society. Of the pacification offering (*shelem;* for the usual translation, see above) shared with the donor, they received the right shank and breast (plate and brisket). Of the purification and penalty offerings, they received everything but the designated fat parts. The whole of the grain offering minus one fistful became theirs.

In addition to food in kind through sacrifices, the tabernacle establishment was provided with other forms of property through votive gifts, which consisted of items sanctified to the use of the tabernacle establishment as part of agreements between individuals and

10. Jacob Milgrom, "The Cultic šggh and its Influence in Psalms and Job," *The Jewish Quarterly Review* 58 (1967): 115–25.
11. Jacob Milgrom, "Sacrifices and offerings, OT," *IDBSupp,* 769.

God. Leviticus 27 lists the forms of votive gifts in the course of
prescribing the rules for assessing the value of an item. Possible gifts
included persons, animals, houses, and land. Persons were valued at
roughly the price they would command in the slave market, then
redeemed at their value. Considering the average wage of a worker
was about one shekel per month, the values were high: as much as
fifty shekels for a man and twenty for a boy.[12] The priest could reduce
the valuation if a laborer had made a vow regarding a person in his
control, like his son or daughter, whose normal valuation was more
than he could pay. Other items could be redeemed at their assessed
value plus one-fifth. The main exception was the votive made under
the special terms of the "ban." Such offerings could not be redeemed,
and in the case of persons were required to be put to death. It is
assumed that only powerful persons could carry out such a vow of
execution, which was of little productive use but of great potential
political value.

In addition to all that the priests received in the form of meat
sacrifices or votive offerings, the priestly establishment and its cult
levied a ten percent tax on all the produce of the land:

> All the tithe of the land, whether of the seed of the land or of the
> fruit of the tree, is Yahweh's. It is holy to Yahweh. If a man wishes
> to redeem any of his tithe, he shall add a fifth to it. All the tithe
> of herds and flocks, every tenth animal of all that pass under the
> herdsman's staff, shall be holy to Yahweh. A man shall not inquire
> whether it is good or bad, neither shall he exchange it; if he ex-
> changes it, then both it and that for which it is exchanged shall be
> holy; it shall not be redeemed. (Lev. 27:30-33, RSV, slightly altered)

This modest tax probably represented by far the most important
source of income to the priestly establishment. It lays down the equivalent of the state tax of the monarchic period. This tax was in addition
to income due to priestly families from the lands they held in private,
which could be extensive. If the random selection of the tithe took
away a particularly valued animal, the owner could redeem his property by paying its assessed value plus a further fifth—or twelve instead
of ten percent on that item.

Although most Judahites were oblivious to the refined theory of
guilt and world order represented in Genesis 1 and explicated throughout the priestly reconstruction of the official temple history, the priests'

12. Gordon J. Wenham, *The Book of Leviticus* (Grand Rapids: Eerdmans, 1979), 338.

social role was consolidated through their privilege of defining guilt. The priests did not necessarily impose guilt for sin. For the cult to foster social order, it was not necessary for the priests to make people feel guilty. People are usually quite prepared to feel they must have done something wrong to bring on their misfortune. What the priests did was to rationalize the expiation of guilt by tying that expiation to a world order. In this sense the priestly cult provided, for those to whom it was accessible, a means of alleviating guilt.

There was nevertheless a momentous negative side to this apparent social good. Although the priestly law called for just adjudication of disputes over debt and land tenure for the benefit of the less powerful, in priestly theory the individual bore primary responsibility for his or her suffering. The majority of those suffering poverty, hunger, and illness took for granted that they were suffering because they were guilty. The theory of guilt attached to the system of sacrifice applied mainly to the guilt of the suffering individual or socially undifferentiated community. There was always a further cost, therefore, to be borne, in addition to the hardship itself.

For the Aaronid cult of the priestly history, settlement of an imbalance cost the people meat. Leviticus 16:30 was basic to the priestly writer's understanding of sacrifice: "Composition (*kpr*, righting of an imbalance) is prerequisite for forgiveness."[13] As for popular theory, the people themselves might prefer to be more fatalistic, and not to assume their own guilt. They also clearly recognized the role of poverty, debt, and indenture in their misery, and looked to the priestly cult for the redress of injustice, for which the priests were also eager to provide a theory, to supplement their use of psalmic prayers.

13. Herbert Chanan Brichto, "On Slaughter and Sacrifice, Blood and Atonement," *Hebrew Union College Annual* 47 (1976): 19–55. The quote is on p. 35.

11

The Creation
of Order

The sixth-century priesthood's overriding interest was in the cult of sacrifice. But in addition to their interest in rules for the tabernacle and its disposition of lifeblood, as a ruling elite the priests were also interested in rules for social justice. Indeed, during the earlier history of the temple priesthood, what the majority of Israelites might have regarded as most distinctive of the priesthood, with its connection to the royal military establishment, was its authority to teach and adjudicate law. No sooner does the book of Leviticus state that it is the function of the priests to distinguish between the holy and the common than it delineates this legislative function: "And you are to teach the people of Israel all the statutes which Yahweh has spoken to them by Moses" (Lev. 10:11).

In the Persian period, the main restriction on the priesthood's power was that Judah was under Persian rule. Persian governors sometimes played the same role as the earlier Judahite kings, and the territory ruled by the temple was smaller than was often the case during the period of the monarchy. Despite this, the absence of a monarchy to compete against in some ways meant that the priesthood wielded even greater power during this period than in earlier periods.

ORDER AND JUSTICE

How did a tradition so preoccupied with cult become so concerned with social justice? The priestly history is a supplement to the Davidic cult history of the founding of the "nation" of Israel. The theme of this history is that God delivered Israel from the injustice of Egypt.

The Exodus provided the basis for the just ordering of life in the land
to which God led his people. Because this history was preserved in
the palace and temple of the long-standing house of David, it came
to be understood as the history of a temple-centered people. The
composers of the priestly history as a matter of course adopted the
view that the foundational history was the history of the origin of
justice in temple-centered Israel.

Not only did the combination of an interest in cult with an interest
in justice not originate with the priestly writer, it went back even
earlier than the earliest documents in the Bible. It is found in some
of the oldest literature in the world from the ancient Near East, dating
from the third millennium B.C.E. And since cults both promulgated
accounts of creation and claimed rights of jurisdiction, it is not at all
surprising to find the association of creation and justice in many parts
of the Bible besides the priestly portions.

In the conception of the priests, the world God created was an
ordered world in which justice prevailed. But when injustice takes
over, the God who created the world can in the course of his judgment
uncreate it. Amos, who like the priestly writers puts cult and justice
together, describes God's act of unmaking the order of creation in the
face of injustice:

> He who made the Pleiades and Orion,
> and turns deep darkness into the morning,
> and darkens the day into night,
> who calls for the waters of the sea,
> and pours them out upon the surface of the earth,
> Yahweh is his name,
> who makes destruction flash forth against the strong,
> so that destruction comes upon the fortress [of the elite]—
> They hate him who reproves in the gate,
> and they abhor him who speaks the truth.
> Therefore, because you trample upon the poor
> and take from him exactions of wheat,
> you have built houses of hewn stone,
> but you shall not dwell in them;
> you have planted pleasant vineyards,
> but you shall not drink their wine.
> For I know how many are your transgressions,
> and how great are your sins—
> you who afflict the righteous,

who take a bribe,
and turn aside the needy in the gate. (Amos 5:8-12)

A similar statement of God's willingness to unmake the created order because of the prevalence of injustice is set forth in Joel:

> The earth quakes before them,
>   the heavens tremble.
> *The sun and moon are darkened,*
>   *and the stars withdraw their shining.*
> Yahweh utters his voice
>   before his enemy,
> for his host is exceedingly great;
>   he that executes his word is powerful.
> For the day of Yahweh is great and very terrible;
>   who can endure it? (Joel 2:10-11)

Jeremiah also wrote of the unmaking of creation as a result of God's anger against injustice:

> I looked on the earth, and lo, *it was waste and void;*
>   *and to the heavens, and they had no light.*
> I looked on the mountains, and lo, they were quaking,
>   and all the hills moved to and fro.
> I looked, and lo, there were no humans,
>   and all the birds of the air had fled.
> I looked, and lo, the fruitful land was a desert,
>   and all its cities were laid in ruins
>   before Yahweh, before his fierce anger.
>   (Jer. 4:23-26 RSV, slightly modified)

Historians usually see in these words of Jeremiah a direct reference to the Jerusalemite priestly tradition of creation, some years before it was put in writing in the precise form seen in Genesis 1. The phrase "waste and void," for example, is identical to "without form and void" (RSV) in the account of creation.

Just as God punishes injustice by undoing the created order, so God recreates order to restore justice:

> In this place of which you say, "It is a waste without human or beast," in the cities of Judah and the streets of Jerusalem that are desolate, without human or ruler or beast, there shall be heard again the voice of mirth and gladness. . . . I shall cause a righteous branch

to spring forth for David, and he shall execute justice and righteousness in the land. . . . David shall never lack a man to sit on the throne . . . and the Levitical priests shall never lack a man in my presence to offer burnt offerings, to burn cereal offerings, and to make my sacrifices for ever. . . . If I have not established *my covenant with day and night and the ordinances of heaven and earth,* then I will reject the descendants of Jacob and David. . . . I will restore their fortunes, and will have mercy upon them. (Jer. 33:10-11, 15, 17-18, 25-26, RSV)

Ezekiel, only slightly younger than Jeremiah, was a Zadokite priest of the temple in Jerusalem at the time of the major deportation of Jerusalemite elite to Babylon in 598 B.C.E. With the fall of the temple in 587 B.C.E, the cult shrine that had been the basis of his existence existed no more. He attributed the fall of his temple to the injustice of the rulers of Judah and Israel, and envisioned a whole new universal and social order, centered on a re-created temple and the return of the priestly *kabod* of God to the temple.

For Ezekiel, as for the priestly writer, the experience of God combined cult and justice. Indeed, he could not even conceive of them as separate, any more than anyone in the ancient world could. When Ezekiel or others of the prophets complained about corruption in the cult, it was not that cult per se was at fault, but that a particular cult participated in the injustice of society and would have to be replaced with a new and purified cult (see, for example, Ezek. 8:1—9:10). Purity and justice are necessary correlates. This is the point of the priestly history and its account of creation, as it is of Amos, Joel, Jeremiah, Ezekiel, and other parts of the Bible.

From the great prophet Jeremiah, to the priest Ezekiel, to no less than the priestly writers of Genesis 1, it is assumed that the ultimate purpose of creation is the establishment of a world order in which justice prevails.[1] Creation, in a word, is the creation of the conditions of justice. This is central to an understanding of Genesis 1.

Although it is concerned for social justice, the priestly revision of the official temple history does not provide a comprehensive treatment of social order. Rather, the revision serves as a vehicle for the priests' ongoing work of sanctioning, interpreting, and executing the laws

1. Both Jeremiah and the priestly history share this view even though they understand the role of the Levites quite differently.

already established in the temple history.[2] As a supplement to an existing set of laws governing social order, it focuses on two particular areas of concern: fair judicial process; and the alleviation of the consequences of debt.

JUDICIAL PROCESS

The concern for fair judicial process is seen in the sacrificial system in the case of the penalty offering:

> If any one sins and commits a breach of faith in a matter of deposit or security, or through robbery, or if he has oppressed his neighbor or has found what was lost and has lied about it, swearing falsely— in any of all the things men do and sin therein, when one has sinned and become guilty, he shall restore what he took by robbery, or what he got by oppression, or the deposit which was committed to him, or the lost thing which he found, or anything about which he has sworn falsely; he shall restore it in full, and shall add a fifth to it, and give it to him to whom it belongs, on the day of his penalty offering. (Lev. 6:2-5, RSV)

The terms of penalty represent the same concern for truth in witness and judgment seen in the liturgies of entrance to the cult in Psalms 15 and 24:

> O God, who shall sojourn in your tent?
> Who shall dwell on your holy hill? Whoever proceeds in
> the plain truth,
> and executes justice,
> and utters the truth in their mind; whoever does not
> slander with the tongue,
> nor make false charge against neighbor; in whose eyes a
> reprobate is despised,
> but who honors those who fear God;
> who swears to their own hurt in trial without flinching,
> who do not put out money at exorbitant interest,
> and who do not take a bribe against the innocent.
> Whoever does these things shall stand fast in the
> sanctuary of God. (Psalm 15)

The rules of justice in the priestly history cluster in the holiness law of Leviticus 17–25. This section of the history may have had a

2. J, E, and possible Proto-deuteronomistic parts of Exodus 20–23 and 34.

life of its own apart from and slightly earlier than the history as a whole, but if so it became an integral part of the official temple scriptures in the early Persian period in Jerusalem. As with the other parts of the history, one scheme lies behind the entire work, with all the parts interrelated to support the priestly conception of justice.

El of the tent, the God of the priestly tabernacle, was characteristically a deliverer of the authoritative word, including the word of judgment. At Ugarit it was said of El:

> Your decree, O El, is wise,
> your wisdom is eternal.
> A life of good fortune your decree.[3]

In line with this character of El, many biblical texts place God at the head of the council of gods:

> God has taken his place in the assembly of El, in the midst of the gods he holds judgment. (Ps. 82:1)[4]

As seen in chapter 7, the holiness law opens with instructions regarding the disposition of lifeblood and regarding intercourse, including incest taboos, avoidance of a menstrual woman, and prohibition of child sacrifice, homosexuality, and bestiality. After a brief reminder of the importance of observing the Sabbath, followed by stipulations regarding the *shelem* sacrifice (the meat feast of the laity), the statutes turn to the subject of the treatment of the disadvantaged, with an emphasis on fair judicial process.

The first concern of the priests is with how those who, unlike themselves, do not own property are to find sustenance. One way this was to be achieved was by allowing the poor to glean the fields at harvest time. This and subsequent laws regarding the hire of day laborers indicates that large estates farmed by hired labor were common in the territory under priestly control:

> When you reap the harvest of your land, you shall not reap your field to its very border, neither shall you gather the gleanings after your harvest. And you shall not strip your vineyard bare, neither

---

3. See Frank M. Cross, *Canaanite Myth and Hebrew Epic* (Cambridge: Harvard University Press, 1973), 184–86.
4. Other examples include 1 Kings 22:5-28, Isa. 6:1-12, and many texts from Isaiah 40–55, beginning with Isa. 40:1-8, with its plural address ("Comfort *ye*") to the assembled deities. See Cross, *Canaanite Myth*, 186-90.

shall you gather the fallen grapes of your vineyard; you shall leave them for the poor and for the resident alien. (Lev. 19:9-10)

You shall not withhold overnight the wages of your day laborer. (19:13)

Do not profane your daughter by making her become a harlot [to alleviate your poverty that comes from having too little or no land], so that the land will not "go harloting. . . ." You shall keep my Sabbaths. (19:29-30)

When an alien [hired worker] resides with you in your land, do not molest him. You shall treat the alien who resides with you the same as the local, and you shall keep the same stipulations ["love"] with him as with yourself. After all, you were aliens in Egypt. (19:33-34)

On the heels of these laws of fair treatment in work, a group of laws stipulates the conduct of judicial process:

You shall not steal, nor dissimulate with or conspire against each other. You shall not swear falsely by my name, and so profane the name of your God. (Lev. 19:11-12)

You shall do no injustice in rendering judgment. You shall not be partial to the poor or defer to the great. With justice you shall render judgment in the cases of your neighbor. (19:15)

Given that the system of land tenure and product distribution was already heavily weighted in favor of the wealthy, it might be supposed that justice required giving the benefit of any doubt to the poor, or even favoring the poor outright. The priestly legislators do not, however, take this position. They adopt instead a concept of justice in which every individual is treated the same regardless of wealth and power:

You shall not go about spreading slander among the people. You shall not stand idly by when the lifeblood of your neighbor is at stake. Harbor no hatred against your brother in your heart. Go ahead and give your neighbor a piece of your mind, just don't bear a grudge to do him wrong some day [since that makes it hard to be impartial in judgment]. *You shall keep the same stipulations ["love"] with your neighbor as with yourself.* (19:16-18)

You shall do no wrong in rendering judgment in matters regarding measures of length, weight, or capacity. You shall have just balances, just weights, a just *ephah*-measure and a just *hin*-measure. (19:35-36)

DEBT EASEMENT

Mixed with further stipulations regarding various taboos based on priestly ideals and the conditions for eating meat and feasting, the laws governing protection of the disadvantaged and just legal process lead into the prominent subject of the alleviation of the consequences of debt through redemption of land put up for security. This subject is covered in Leviticus 25, the climactic law of those laws based explicitly on the holiness of God in the priestly history.[5]

Peasants living on the margin of subsistence in a land where drought is common—on average every two or three years—found it easy to fall into debt. If they had to eat all their seed due to a low harvest, it meant borrowing to buy seed to plant the next fall. Taxes, rents, fees, charges, interest, and fines were excessive. For security, peasants would put up their ox or ass if they had one, their own bodies as slave labor for a given period of time, the body of a daughter in prostitution, or their land.

Custom and law in Palestine periodically prescribed ways to alleviate the hardship caused by the loss of such securities. For example, a law the priestly history absorbed from an earlier revision[6] of the official temple history ruled that a person could be forced to serve as a debt slave at most for a period of seven years. Less than a century earlier than the priestly history was composed, a law from the time of Josiah,[7] probably not one absorbed by the writers of the priestly history, considered the consequences of the emancipation of a slave after seven years and ruled that loans made had to be remitted in a fixed seventh year, the "year of remission" of debt (Deut. 15:1-18). This presumably involved the return of securities as well.

The law of remission was a practice with an already ancient history by the time of the priesthood that conceived of Genesis 1 and its attendant laws. But this practice was reinterpreted by the sixth-century

5. For the background and purpose of such laws, which play a very important role throughout the Bible, see Marvin L. Chaney, "Debt Easement in Old Testament History and Tradition," in *The Bible and the Politics of Exegesis: Essays in Honor of Norman K. Gottwald,* ed. David Jobling and others (New York: Pilgrim Press, 1991).
6. From E.
7. A Deuteronomistic law.

priests. The remission of debt and restoration of security, whether labor or real estate, was reassigned to the forty-ninth year:

> You shall make sacred the 49th,[8] and proclaim liberty throughout the land to all its inhabitants.[9] It shall be a *jubilee* [*yobel*] for you, when each of you shall return to his property and each of you shall return to his family estate. A *jubilee* shall that 49th year be to you; in it you shall neither sow, nor reap what grows of itself, nor gather the grapes from the undressed vines. For it is a *jubilee*; it shall be holy to you; you shall eat what it yields out of the field. In this *jubilee* year, each of you shall return to his own property. (Lev. 25:10-13).[10]

The word translated "liberty" is *deror,* meaning manumission or emancipation. It is cognate with the terms *duraru* and *anduraru* in Mesopotamia. All these terms refer to a law to prevent the permanent alienation of certain possessions, especially real property. There was no provision for free redemption prior to the 49th year.[11] For a person whose property was bonded a long time after a previous jubilee, this did not represent such a burden. But the difference between seven and forty-nine years is a significant one. The whole forty-nine years was longer than the lifespan of many peasants.[12]

The promulgation of the law of jubilee was a normal part of a periodic reform law that in Mesopotamia was called *misharu*—a royal reform act usually with *duraru,* a decree of remission, as one of its main components. One historian describes the practice of such reform acts as follows:

> In the first full year of his reign a king proclaimed a *misharum*. This act consisted mainly of remissions of specific kinds of debts and obligations, the remission to be in effect for a limited time only. Along with provisions of this kind there might have been some

8. The text says "fiftieth." Nearly everyone agrees that this designation would include the previous *jubilee*.
9. This is the text that appears on the Liberty Bell near Independence Hall in Philadelphia. In the King James Version: "Proclaim liberty throughout all the land unto all the inhabitants thereof."
10. The only reference to *jubilee* outside of Leviticus 25 and 27 is in Num. 36:4. The situation and stipulation in inheritance law described there is thought to postdate the promulgation of Leviticus 25 in P.
11. Paid redemption was provided for.
12. The copy of North's *Sociology of the Biblical Jubilee* available during the writing of this book had in it a sheet of notepaper left by a student reader, on which the student had perceptively written, "But who could expect to live for 50 years in those days?"

procedural provisions of a more permanent nature. . . . The proclamation of the *misharum* was not necessarily accompanied by the
issuing of a formal text containing all the provisions of the act. The
"meat" of the act—i.e., the remissive provisions—was probably
diffused through the realm by official correspondence from the royal
chancery. . . . The *misharum*-act . . . was not only a vital force in
the economic life of the Old Babylonian period . . . but they con-
stituted the best justification for the kings' claims to have been
sharru misharim ["kings of just rule"], and served perhaps as the
primary inspirational source for the growth of the "law-code" type
of inscription. . . . *Anduraram shakanum* ["establish freedom"] is one
of the most frequent phrases applied to the *misharum*-acts in date-
formulae and inscriptions. . . . It would seem that *misharum* is the
more general term, while *andurarum* was a more specific word for
"release" or "return" of persons held in bondage for debt or real
estate so held.[13]

Such enactments were not limited to the ruler's first year, but could
be made at any time, as long as not too frequently.

Royal edicts of this kind were promulgated in Israel before the time
of the priestly writer. For instance, when Jeremiah threatened King
Zedekiah with God's anger during Nebuchadnezzar's final siege of
Jerusalem in 588 B.C.E., Zedekiah responded, under the pressure of
events, by declaring "freedom" in Judah:

> The word which came to Jeremiah from Yahweh, after King Zed-
> ekiah had made a covenant with all the people in Jerusalem to make
> a proclamation of liberty to them, that every one should set free
> his Hebrew slaves, male and female, so that no one should enslave
> a Judahite, his brother. And they obeyed, all the princes and all the
> people who had entered into the covenant that every one would
> set free his slave, male or female, so that they would not be enslaved
> again. They obeyed and set them free. But afterward they turned
> around and took back the male and female slaves they had set free,
> and brought them into subjection as slaves.
>
> The word of Yahweh came to Jeremiah: Thus says Yahweh, the
> God of Israel: I made a covenant with your ancestors when I brought
> them out of the land of Egypt, out of the house of slavery, saying,
> "At the end of six years each of you must set free the fellow Hebrew
> who has been sold to you and has served you six years; you must

13. J. J. Finkelstein, "Ammiṣaduqa's Edict and the Babylonian 'Law Codes,' " *Journal of Cuneiform Studies* 15 (1961): 102–4.

set him free from your service." But your ancestors did not listen to me or incline their ears to me. You recently repented and did what was right in my eyes by proclaiming liberty, each to his neighbor, and you made a covenant before me in the temple called by my name; but then you turned around and profaned my name when each of you took back his male and female slaves, whom you had set free according to their desire, and you brought them into subjection to be your slaves. Therefore, thus says Yahweh: You have not obeyed me by proclaiming liberty . . . ; thus I am about to proclaim to you liberty to the sword, to pestilence, and to famine. (Jer. 34:8-17 RSV, slightly modified)

Zedekiah's enactment of liberty (*deror*) seems to be regarded as an unscheduled royal act, like the *misharu* in Mesopotamia. The special edict of liberty functioned as a royal reform act to rectify a standing injustice. The reference to covenant suggests the ruler required the agreement of the lords and wealthy peasants of his realm to make the edict work. These slave owners reneged on their agreement with Zedekiah. The incident indicates that in Jeremiah's time the law limiting debt slavery in Judah to seven years (Exod. 21:1; compare Deut. 15:1) was theoretically in effect, but was not being kept.

An Old Babylonian text first published twenty years ago illustrates an attempt by a landowner in Mesopotamia, more than a thousand years before Jeremiah or the priestly writer, to avoid losing land the royal officials were determined to release. The text is a petition protesting a decision by an official that hinged on the question of the relevance to a particular instance of a royal reform edict (*misharu*) enacted for the city of Sippar and its lands.[14] The petitioner is appealing to the king to uphold his dispensation from the edict. The tablet on which this text is written is much eroded in the middle sections, hence the missing words in places:

When my lord raised high the Golden Torch[15] for Sippar, instituting the *misharum* for Shamash [the Mesopotamian Sun god, the chief god of Sippar] who loves him, and convened in Sippar the "secretary of infantry,"[16] the judges of Babylon and the judges of Sippar, they

14. J. J. Finkelstein, "Some New *Misharum* Material and Its Implications," in *Studies in Honor of Benno Landsberger* (Assyriological Studies, 16) (Chicago: University of Chicago Press, 1965), 233–46. The translation is taken essentially from p. 236.
15. An expression for enacting an edict of *misharu*.
16. Apparently some kind of sheriff.

reviewed the cases of the citizens of Sippar, "heard" the tablets of
purchase of field, house, and orchard, and ordered broken those in
which the land was to be released[17] by the terms of the *misharum*.
Three units of improved real estate inside a district of Sippar which,
according to their original contract, were purchased . . . in the
year. . . . That house. . . . I and the owner of . . . and the judges
. . . the tablets of purchase . . . according to . . . they broke.[18] I
took my tablets to the assembly; Rish-Shamash, the presiding officer
of Sippar, Kudiya the administrator, and Sin-nadin-shumi, the records secretary, reviewed my tablets and affirmed them. They then
sent them to the house of Shalimtehushu the "captain of barbers."[19]
Without giving me a hearing, he broke my tablets in Sippar. Upon
being informed, and in consternation, I collected the pieces of my
tablets from his house and showed them to Rish-Shamash, Kudiya,
and Sin-nadin-shumi, but they said, "What can we say to the 'captain
of barbers'?" To you, O divine one, I have therefore come. Let my
lord offer me the ruling in the case of the breaking of tablets in the
absence of judges and of the principal party to the case.

Although periodic remission of debt, release of debt slaves, and
return of land held in security for debt was already an ancient practice
in the world of the priestly writer of Genesis 1 and Leviticus 25, the
priestly jubilee (*yobel*), like the seventh year of remission, is distinctive
in that it is a permanently scheduled decree rather than an occasional
one based on the ad hoc edict of the king (*misharu*). The permanent
nature of the jubilee and its scheduling every forty-nine years was
based on the numerical patterning of the priestly conception of creation, but it served a practical purpose. Since the Jerusalemite priesthood in the Persian period could not claim the *royal* prerogative to
enact reform edicts on an ad hoc basis, they followed the lead of the
Israelite custom of permanent periodic debt remission and formulated
their own version of it.[20]

The priests explicitly state the theory that God is the final owner
of land and slaves: "The land shall not be sold in perpetuity, for the

17. Literally "pass out," exactly as in the Hebrew of Lev. 25:28.
18. About 12 lines are missing or damaged. It seems that the petitioner was able to procure new
tablets of purchase showing the terms of ownership.
19. He is apparently the head of a contingent of city or palace guards, not of barbers in the literal
sense.
20. The vision in Isa. 61:1-2 of the restoration of justice through the proclamation of a year of
release, written probably during the fifth century B.C.E., seems to imply again the more ancient
and common ad hoc proclamation. The anointing referred to may even allude to a royal anointing.

land is mine. . . . The people of Israel are my slaves whom I brought out of Egypt" (Lev. 25:23, 55). On this basis, God rules to protect the social and economic stability based on the stability of an extended family's tenure of real property. Neither land nor labor shall be sold in perpetuity.

Land sold to cover a debt could be redeemed by the original seller or another member of the family at any time during the forty-nine years it was allowed to be held as security. What was sold, therefore, was not the land, but the use of it for a certain period of time. When sold or redeemed, its price of redemption was figured on a prorated basis:

> In this jubilee year each of you shall return to his property. If you sell to your neighbor or buy from your neighbor, you shall not wrong one another. According to the number of years after the [last] jubilee, you shall buy from your neighbor, and according to the number of years [before the next jubilee] for crops he shall sell to you. If the years are many you shall increase the price, and if the years are few you shall diminish the price, for it is the number of crops that he is selling to you. . . . If your brother becomes poor, and sells part of his property, then his next of kin shall come and redeem what his brother has sold. If a man has no one to redeem it, and then himself becomes prosperous, and finds sufficient means to redeem it, let him reckon the years since he sold it and pay back the overpayment to the man to whom he sold it; and he shall then return his property. But if he has not sufficient means to get it back for himself, then what he sold shall remain in the hand of him who bought it until the jubilee year; in the jubilee it shall be released, and he shall return to his property. (Lev. 25:13-16, 25-28 RSV, slightly modified)

The purpose of the jubilee was to protect mainly the lands and homes of the bulk of the population, the villagers, from permanent dispossession. Property within a walled city—the urban property of the relatively wealthy—was excluded from the provision of the jubilee. It could be redeemed within a year of sale, but after that it belonged to the new owner in perpetuity.

Even though the year of release was shifted from the seventh to the forty-ninth year, the concept of rest in the seventh year did not disappear altogether. Rather, the seventh year became a year of rest for the land. As the manna collected on the sixth day sufficed for the seventh day during Israel's wilderness trek, so also no food was to be harvested every seventh year. The food harvested in the sixth year was to suffice for the seventh year and even the eighth, since without working to grow food in the seventh there was none available until a full half-year after work had recommenced:

> If you say, "What shall we eat in the seventh year, if we may not sow or gather in our crop?" I will command my blessing upon you in the sixth year, so that it will bring forth fruit for three years. When you sow in the eighth year, you will be eating old produce; until the ninth year, when its produce comes in, you shall eat the old. (Lev. 25:20-22, RSV)

This plan rarely if ever matched the weather of Palestine, which was just as likely to produce a drought in the sixth year as to produce a bumper harvest. It was typical priestly theory tying the cycle of Sabbath land rests to creation, and its net result was to inflict further hardship on the poor.

The implication that resting the land resulted in a rest for workers in bondage who would normally perform work on the land, so that such workers might as well be released, is not drawn. In fact, the change from a seventh year of debt remission to a seventh year of fallow and agricultural moratorium represents a notable loss in protection of the poor. In addition, if agricultural work were to cease every seventh year, it can be imagined that for that year and the next, and a year or two before and after, food prices would increase markedly. It is difficult to avoid the impression that the Sabbath year of fallow exacerbated the indebted condition of the poor, making the legislated release of the forty-ninth year all the more essential.

In the next section of the law, the jubilee legislation anticipates the calamity of skyrocketing food prices brought on by the Sabbath year cessation of agriculture. Even assuming the harvest of the sixth year was a good one, it would be reasonable to expect that many people would not be able to save enough food from the sixth year to tide them over to the ninth and would thus be forced to pay money for food to those who controlled large stores, including the Jerusalemite priestly class themselves. In this situation, the priests enjoin public benefaction:

> If your brother becomes poor [in relation to the skyrocketing cost of food], and cannot maintain himself with you, you shall maintain

> him; extend to him the privileges of an alien or a tenant, so that
> he may continue to live with you. Do not extract interest from him
> in either money or kind. . . . You are to lend him neither money
> at interest nor food at profit. (Lev. 25:35-37, NAB)

Why the priests enjoined charity in cases of poverty resulting from
the seventh-year land rest may be discerned from the custom of local
men of wealth supplying food to the populace in times of need in
ancient Greece and most of the cities under Roman rule. Besides
serving to ameliorate conditions that might sow seeds of rebellion, it
was an excellent way for a local lord to strengthen the bonds of
patronage between himself and the people whose popular support he
cultivated. Under such circumstances charity might have its limits,
however, and the likely consequence would be for poor persons to
be forced into debt to provide food for themselves or their families.

THE LAWS IN EFFECT

As a part of the priestly desire to limit the influence of outside patrons
over Judahite lands, the rules for bonded service distinguished Judahites, or native Palestinians, from aliens:

> When your countryman becomes so impoverished that he sells you
> his services, do not make him work as a slave. Rather let him be
> like a hired servant or like your tenant, working with you until the
> jubilee year, when he, together with his children, shall be released
> from your service and return to his kindred and to the property of
> his ancestors. . . . Slaves, male and female, you may indeed possess,
> provided you buy them from among the neighboring nations. You
> may also buy them from among the aliens who reside with you
> and from their children who are born and reared in your land. Such
> slaves you may own as chattels, and leave to your sons as hereditary
> property, making them perpetual slaves. (Lev. 25:39-46, NAB)

Judahites who became slaves to aliens could be redeemed at any point
for the usual price prorated to the jubilee.

The distinction between Judahite and alien was important to the
priesthood of the Persian period. Their temple-based prerogatives of
provincial taxation, control of the disposition of land, and regulation
of trade were continually being encroached upon by economic and
political forces in Palestine that were aligned more with the Greek
sphere of influence than with Persia. When during the fifth century

B.C.E. the Aaronids went increasingly over to the Greek side, there were parties of priests who remained loyal to Persian authority and who therefore continued to have an interest in distinguishing native Judahites, who owed allegiance to Persia and hence the temple in Jerusalem, from non-Judahites, who owed no such allegiance.

Given this distinction and the privileges accorded Judahites, it was also clearly imperative for a Judahite family to maintain, or have maintained, good records of their family background and inherited rights to the use of their land. The keeping of genealogical records was a primary function of the Jerusalemite priests in their role as clerics in the society. Their status in this role became all the greater with the importance of the distinction between Judahite and non-Judahite.

The power of estate owners in Judah was clearly greater under the proxy rule of the priesthood than during most periods under royalty. In the cases of Jeroboam in Exodus 21:1, Josiah in Deuteronomy 15:1, and later the Aaronid priests, it was apparently necessary to establish a rule for periodic remission because they did not have the power to enforce a decree of liberty (*misharu*) as an ad hoc royal or central government decree.

It was an advantage to Persian rule to control local major land owners in Judah in some way, but their control through the law of debt remission, to the disadvantage of major landowners, was limited, and during most of the Persian period the Persians had difficulty maintaining their authority in Palestine. The enforcement of the law of remission would work to the benefit of the temple, which represented central control in relation to the decentralized control of non-Jerusalemite local lords in Judah and its vicinity. The assumption that a declaration of a year of remission would work in favor of the temple is displayed clearly in Third Isaiah (Isaiah 56–66), which in elaborate terms envisions the restoration of the wealth and influence of the temple in Jerusalem through several procedures, not least of which is an edict of liberty (*deror*):

> The spirit of the lord Yahweh is upon me, because Yahweh has anointed me to bring good news to the poor; he has sent me to bind the wounds of the discouraged, to proclaim liberty [*deror*] to the captives, an opening up to those who are bound; to proclaim

the year of Yahweh's favor [for the debtor], and the day of victory
of our God. (Isa. 61:1-2)[21]

Even though these lines in their rhetorical context refer to the return
of expatriate and exiled Judahites as well as to the release of the poor,
the implication is clear within the context of the whole of Third Isaiah
that an edict of liberty would contribute great material benefits to the
temple. The same can be assumed for the priestly law of jubilee.

By laying down the remission of debt, the manumission of slaves,
and the protection of long-term family tenure rights, the law of jubilee
in theory represents an important principle of liberation. However,
the distinction between native Judahite and alien non-Judahite, the
lengthy extension of the period of land loss from six to forty-eight
years, and the predictable rise in food prices due to the cessation of
agriculture for one year every seven years in practice represents a
significant compromising of the principle of liberation as it might
ideally be conceived.[22]

The distance between practice and ideal is the result of the way in
which the Aaronid priesthood viewed themselves as an elite ruling
class, based upon their understanding of the created order as set forth
in Genesis 1. Viewing themselves as little less than gods with dominion
over the creation, it was inevitable that any reinterpretation of the
centuries-old custom of remission would serve to enhance their own
status.

---

21. See also Nehemiah 5.
22. This is not to judge the priestly law by modern standards, but simply to point out the
difference between the law and the ideal as frequently presented in modern literature.

12

The Priestly Account
in the New Testament

The priestly service of sacrifice, coupled with the service of musical prayer and praise by the Levites, continued to be carried out for centuries in the second temple of the Persian period. The dominant families of the priestly class also remained in power from one century to another.

Following the Babylonian detention of many of their leaders, the Judahites of Palestine were allowed relative autonomy, retaining their religious identity. The Davidic state was severely compromised, however, since no on-site monarchy was permitted. Without a functioning monarch, the interpretation of the Torah had become the focus of Judahite identity, and hence the scribal class became the central figures in the task of maintaining and even enlarging the autonomy the Judahites were permitted to exercise. The Persians, Greeks, and Romans usually fostered local group identity, as Moscow did for decades with the peoples under Soviet sway, as a means of keeping the people under control.

But there are always individuals and groups who want more than local group identity and political concessions. They want a political identity and greater political power as well. As the generations wore on, two significant changes took place in the temple cult. The first was the development of a new monarchy, centered on the temple, under the Maccabees. The second was a great new temple.

THE MACCABEES
The Greeks had finally won their contest with the Persians in Palestine, when Alexander conquered the East in the late fourth century B.C.E.

Alexander's empire in the east split in two, under the Ptolemies in Egypt and the Seleucids in Syria. During the third century Palestine came under Ptolemaic rule. In 198 B.C.E. the Seleucids defeated the Ptolemies and Palestine became theirs.

Even before the decisive battle, the Seleucid king Antiochus III had encouraged Judahite dissatisfaction with Ptolemaic rule. When he took over in Jerusalem, he waived taxes for everyone for three years, and for the temple and priests forever. But in the face of the threat of Rome from the west, the Seleucids were soon forced to reverse their policy of leniency and even to resort to robbing local temples to supplement their state resources.

Some powerful families in Judah supported Seleucid policies. Antiochus IV played these families off against each other by putting the office of high priest up for sale to the highest bidder. First one family held the position, then another. But when Seleucid advances in Egypt were stopped in 169 B.C.E., Antiochus IV decided to strengthen his boundary zone with Egypt by making Jerusalem a Hellenistic city with Hellenistic customs and laws. He broke down the walls of the city, established a garrison of Seleucid troops, and resettled the city with a mixed Judahite and alien population loyal to the Seleucids.

For several reasons, including one high priest's need to prove his favor with the Seleucids, the Hellenistic faction initiated a suppression of Judahite custom and practice, which included suspending the temple law, replacing temple sacrifice with sacrifices to Zeus, and forbidding the rites of circumcision and the keeping of Sabbath. These policies were backed up by the reinforced Seleucid garrison in Jerusalem.

Against such policies many Judahites joined the rebellion led by the priest Mattathias and his sons, known as the Maccabees after the nickname of one of the sons. The war for Jerusalem lasted three years. In 164 B.C.E. the Maccabees captured Jerusalem and rededicated the temple for service according to the ancestral priestly law. A moderate high priest was appointed, but the struggle against the foreign power did not subside. Backed by Rome, the Maccabees carried on the fight with a view to independence. Jonathan of the Maccabees was soon in control of much of Palestine and was able to use his power to secure the high priesthood for himself in 152. By 150 Jonathan was so powerful that he began to support the Seleucids in their efforts to quash revolts in other places. Under Simon, Jonathan's brother and

successor, the Maccabees became the holders of both the high priesthood and hereditary sovereignty in Palestine. The dynasty was called
Hasmonean, after an ancestor of Mattathias. The Hasmonean family
had whipped up a revolt and ended up restoring the Judahite kingdom.

In the period 140–76 B.C.E., the Hasmoneans expanded their kingdom until it became nearly as large as David's kingdom nine hundred
years before. The sphere of influence of the temple and Hasmonean
priesthood grew along with the Hasmonean kingdom. A group of
priests identified with the venerable but displaced Aaronid priesthood
departed Jerusalem and began a community on the Dead Sea to keep
alive their traditions and claims to office. These were the sectarians
at Qumran and probably other localities nearby. The Hasmoneans
kept their connections with Rome as they grew in strength. It was
difficult to distinguish the Hasmonean kingdom from other Hellenistic
kingdoms.

Over the decades, the Judahite state became increasingly Hellenized
in administration and military organization. The autocrat John Hyrcanus, who ruled from 135 to 104 B.C.E., led this development. He
gave his sons Greek names. Like many other Palestinian monarchs
before him, including David, he hired Greek and other Mediterranean
mercenaries, and thus reduced his dependence on local military support.

It was under Hyrcanus that an apparent party of devout Judahites,
who were descended from earlier pietists and were put off by the
propensity of the Maccabean successors to take on the trappings of
Hellenistic monarchy, came into conflict with the ruling regime. These
opponents represented the beginnings of the later Pharisees, though
their exact relationship is not yet fully understood. The ruling house
of the Maccabees became increasingly powerful as their conquests
added ever more territory to their tax base. Some Judahites benefited
from this new Jerusalemite wealth, but most did not. When some of
these proto-Pharisees called on Hyrcanus to surrender the high priesthood and relinquish the sanction of the temple for Maccabean ag-
grandizement, the monarch looked for support among a group called
the Sadducees, among the new priestly beneficiaries of the Hasmonean
rise to power.

The Sadducees thus became the primary patrons and beneficiaries
of the cult system based on Genesis 1 and the rest of the priestly
conception of the created order. The majority of Judahites opposed

their rule. Civil war flared during the reign of Alexander Jannaeus. The popular party, led by the Pharisees, called on Seleucid help to oust Alexander. Some Judahites hesitated, however, at the prospect of the Seleucids back in power in Jerusalem and transferred their loyalty to Alexander. Once in control, he crucified hundreds of Pharisees in revenge.

The coming to power under renewed monarchic conditions of a new group of families to fill the roles of the Jerusalemite priestly class, under circumstances in which they were the objects of great unpopularity, was the first significant change in the priesthood of the second temple. The second change, the renewed expansion of the temple and the role of its priesthood under Herod the Great and his immediate successors, was an outgrowth of the first.

As Roman influence in Palestine increased, two sons of Alexander and his queen Salome Alexandra vied for power. One son was Aristobulus. The weaker, Hyrcanus, was supported by the Idumean sheikh Antipater, the father of Herod. In 63 B.C.E., these two appealed for support to the Roman general Pompey. A party of populists, led perhaps by Pharisees, requested Pompey not to recognize either. Pressed by the rivals, Pompey took Jerusalem, beginning Roman control over Palestine that would last almost seven hundred years. He deported Aristobulus to Rome and appointed Hyrcanus high priest but not king, thus ending the Hasmonean kingdom. The long-standing Roman support for the Hasmoneans had come home to roost.

HEROD THE GREAT AND THE NEW TEMPLE

Anthony made Herod puppet king of the Judahites in 40 B.C.E., thereby initiating the Herodian dynasty, which ruled on and off until the fall of the temple in 70 C.E. Herod recaptured Jerusalem from the Parthians in 37 B.C.E. and ruled there on behalf of Rome until 4 B.C.E.

Claimants to the kingdom went under the code word "messiah" (in Greek, "christ"). The way a claimant could make his claim most tangible was to reestablish the temple. A wealthy king with the backing of the most powerful state the world had yet known, Herod the Great began a major building program rivaling the great Solomon in grandeur. Until quite recently most of the antiquities protruding above ground in Palestine were constructed by Herod. He ordered the temple greatly expanded in a project so ambitious that it took nearly a hundred years to complete. This magnificent temple stood on a giant platform, whose foundations are still to be seen in the platform of the Haram esh-Sharif, the temple mount on which stands the Dome of the Rock, in Jerusalem today.

With the enlargement of the temple came the expansion of the wealth and influence of the Sadducees. In the nominal kingdom of the Judahites headed by Herod and, with breaks in continuity, his sons, the temple once again came into its own as the prime focus of Judahites far and wide. Expatriate Judahites in the cities of the Roman and Parthian empires, by now outnumbering their compatriots in Palestine, likewise looked to the temple for leadership, direction, and identity, thus adding to its status.

The new opportunities for advancement made possible by the rise of the Hasmoneans made individual leaders and families wealthy who not long before played no significant public role at all.[1] The old aristocracy had been heavily disenfranchised and discredited by the Hasmonean usurpation, particularly after the new ruling house joined the office of high priest with that of king. The expansion of the Hasmoneans offered their retainers and supporters the chance to grow rich in Jerusalem-controlled trade and landholdings. This new aristocracy became known as the Sadducees, adopting the traditional Zadokite label. For several generations their main struggle was against the displaced priestly aristocracy of the pre-Maccabean era. By the time of Herod, however, they found themselves locked in a duel primarily with the so-called Pharisees, the populist proponents of legal and ritual purity and close adherence to the stipulations of the temple scriptures.

Under Herod and his sons, even the new Hasmonean elite lost their status. As a Roman puppet, Herod appointed his own new aristocracy, or Sadducees, usually from outside Palestine altogether, especially from the important Judahite families of Alexandria and Babylonia. Herod's generals included Greeks from many localities, but rarely local Palestinian leaders. The priestly offices of the temple changed hands often among four rival families, so that no one household could challenge Herod's position. From 40 B.C.E. to 60 C.E., therefore, the new temple authorities, with few if any social ties in

1. Norman K. Gottwald, *The Hebrew Bible: A Socio-Literary Introduction* (Philadelphia: Fortress Press, 1985), 448–51.

Palestine, became unable to fulfill their basic social responsibility of maintaining law and order in behalf of the Roman occupation.[2]

The Romans promoted Herod and his family to keep down revolt, but eventually the Judahites attempted rebellion under a number of different claimants to the throne, referred to in Mark's Gospel as false messiahs, all of whom were eventually discredited by the failure of their attempts to create a sovereign Judahite state. As far as most Judahites were concerned, Jesus of Nazareth was just one such discredited messiah, and his followers made little headway among the Judahites because their messiah did not establish Israel as an independent state.

THE END OF THE TEMPLE

In a major revolt against Roman forces in Palestine, the temple was brought down in 70 C.E., and with it the nearly 200-year-old prerogatives of various Sadducean families. The focal point of Judahite loyalty and identity—the temple and its attendant elite priesthood—no longer existed. Consequently the priestly revision of the Pentateuch, which had been transmitted as the chief temple scriptures, could no longer refer, as it had since its composition in the sixth century B.C.E., simply to the temple and its service. If Judahite identity as conceived in the temple scriptures was to survive, the scriptures would have to be given a significantly new interpretation.

There were many different sects and parties among the Judahites of the early first century C.E. There were the temple elite, the priesthood, including the great landed families, the Sadducees. The Pharisees were a local, scribal clergy, outside Jerusalem. There were also ascetics who set themselves apart to await the arrival of God, notably Essenes at Qumran. And there were revolutionaries who believed in forcing God's hand to reconstitute the Davidic kingdom. Indeed, there were three distinct groups of Zealots among the many different factions vying for the throne when the revolution occurred in 67–70 C.E.

Throughout the Roman Empire there were adherents to the various interpretations of Torah that guided these Palestinian groups. Up to ten percent of the empire was Judean by religion, and nearly all of these people lived in urban communities. In Alexandria, a fifth of the

2. Martin Goodman, *The Ruling Class of Judaea: The Origins of the Jewish Revolt Against Rome A.D. 66–70* (Cambridge: Cambridge University Press, 1987).

population was Judean, while forty-five thousand are estimated to have lived in Antioch of Syria. Judeans all over the empire took their religious identity from the leaders of the different groups in Palestine, many of them sending money for the upkeep of the temple or contributing to the cause of Palestine's liberation. The dispersal of the Judeans to the far-flung corners of the world had been going on a long time, even before the Babylonian exile, and certainly after that episode. The elite formed a trading network in cities all over the map—a network maintained by allegiance to the temple. It was upon this temple-centered network that the homogeneity of their communities was founded, so that to lose one's religion was to lose one's worldwide economic and social contacts.

When the temple, the basis of Judean identity, was removed, the factions that survived were those that had a replacement for the temple "ready to go." The Essenes, who had banked on the end of the present world order, were eliminated; the Sadducees were decimated; the Zealots were discredited, their revolution having failed. Of the many ways of following Judean tradition in the pre-70 C.E. period, two were best adapted to survive under the circumstances of unrelenting imperial rule over the Judeans.

The temple scriptures sanctioned and dealt with Judean jurisdiction and legal rights within the framework of imperial jurisdiction. These rights pertained to the state or provincial level of jurisdiction, represented by the temple. With the fall of the temple, it was necessary to reinterpret the scriptures so that their concern for rights could be understood at a different level of jurisdiction. Instead of the temple itself, the reinterpretation of the temple scriptures formed the center of Judean identity. Two different reinterpretations were promulgated by what became, during the two hundred years or so after the destruction of the temple, two rival groups, the Jews and the Christians.

The crushing defeat by Rome put an end to any hopes of a sense of regional identity based on autonomy. The state or provincial level of jurisdiction ceased to be an option. This left the Judeans to choose between the identity enjoyed at the local level of jurisdiction in the towns and villages of Palestine (and from that center farther abroad), or the identity afforded by life in the cities of the Roman Empire. Those known to us after 70 C.E. as the Jews were those Judeans who, as heirs of the Pharisees, found a new identity in an institution that adapted the scriptures for use at the level of local and regional life in

the villages and towns of Palestine, where life went on largely un-
changed. Those known to us as the Christians were those Judeans
and others who, as heirs of the followers of Jesus of Nazareth, found
their identity in an institution that adapted the scriptures for use at
the level of the imperial cities. Their goal was nothing less than the
conversion of the empire. This was a decisive move that was to catapult
both the Jewish and Christian movements from small Judean groups
to major world religions.

The key to the survival of these groups is to be found in their
response to conditions in Palestine during the whole of the Herodian
period. Each group held the temple to be important, but due for
purification. Neither group respected the Sadducees and their conduct
of the spiritual life of society. They had a critical but expectant attitude
toward the temple. They wanted to see the temple operated along
lines other than those followed by the Sadducees, with whom they
had had an uneasy relationship for as long as the Sadducees had existed.

JEWS AND CHRISTIANS

After 70 C.E., the Jews hoped for the restoration of the temple, but
their immediate concern was the keeping of the stipulations of the
Torah. These stipulations included those of the sixth-century B.C.E.
priesthood, with the exception of the sacrificial laws pertaining to the
temple. Observance of Torah was viewed as a means of repurification
of the land of Palestine. But since the Old Testament per se was no
longer culturally "alive" because of loss of the temple, Jewish religious
leaders and scribes based in the cities and towns of Palestine, known
as rabbis, interpreted how Torah was to be applied in the absence of
the temple. Their interpretation of Torah for the current needs of the
Jews is found in the Mishnah, which became the living scriptures in
rabbinic Judaism from the end of the second century.

The rabbis did not immediately achieve preeminence in their post-
70 C.E. setting, however. During the second century, they struggled
for leadership with the chief families of the Galilean synagogues, the
wealthy landowners who took over the patronage positions vacated
by the discredited and disenfranchised Sadducees. And because Judaism centered on the villages, it took several hundred years for the
Mishnah gradually to reach Judeans all over the world and become
accepted as the definition of what it means to be Judean. The Talmud,

the final interpretation of the Mishnah, was not completed in one form until the fourth or fifth century C.E.

What became the Christian side came to be identified with the irrevocable loss of the temple. In the pre-70 period, the groups who became Christians had often participated in the cult of the temple, held the temple to be a significant part of their identity, and expected their messiah to return and rule at the temple. But their critical views toward the corrupt temple institution managed by the Sadducees, coupled with their geographical distance from it in the case of the many Christian cells in cities throughout the empire, meant that once the temple had been destroyed by the Romans, Christian writers could represent their view of scripture in a way that excluded the temple altogether. They reinterpreted the temple scriptures to show that the temple service and its priesthood were not what the Pentateuch was ever really about.

This reinterpretation of the role of the temple was championed by, among others, an expatriate Judean by the name of Paul of Tarsus. A Roman citizen, well before the crisis of 70 C.E., he had helped to set up an urban network throughout the empire, against strong opposition from his Judean peers in Palestine, which now proved to be an important key to the survival of the group. Paul's writings were selected to form a large portion of the Christian scriptures because he proved to be the preeminent theoretician of the view that one could be a Christian apart from Palestine or the temple. Before 70 C.E. Paul had been only barely tolerated by the Christian church's leaders. The Judeans accused him of violating the temple, and a certain Stephen before him had been stoned to death for demonstrating that the Torah does not refer to the temple. Most of the other literary works in the New Testament were included for similar reasons. For instance, Luke-Acts distinguishes sharply between the temple and Christianity. The letter to the Ephesians might well be described as a twenty-ninth chapter of Acts because it shows how the temple has been superseded by the Christian community. In this letter, probably not written by Paul, the writer appeals to Caesar, just as at the end of Luke-Acts. But instead of claiming his innocence against the Judeans, the writer instead asks Caesar to take a look at the supposed peace that prevails between alien and Judean in the Mediterranean Christian communities as an example of how imperial peace might come about. In other words, both Luke-Acts and Ephesians are reinterpretations of Paul's

letters for the post–70 C.E. situation. Mark's Gospel became the basis
of still other Gospels because it too deals with the destruction of the
temple and its replacement by the Christian community.

Perhaps the basic distinction between the two surviving Judean
forms of scriptural faith and institutional allegiance was how they
viewed the temple. The one group continued to value the temple as
essential to their identity, even though it no longer functioned. The
other group dispensed with the temple altogether and regarded it as
justly and irremediably condemned.

After 70 C.E. the Christian groups were able to interpret much that
had been thought and said before 70 C.E. as though it referred to the
condemnation of the temple and the end of its value for adherents to
the Jerusalemite scriptures. It is necessary to distinguish between what
was done and written before 70 C.E. that was later interpreted in terms
of the fall of the temple from what was done or said after the fall.

JESUS

Jesus himself seems to have identified with what in scripture is the
prophetic perspective more than the temple priestly. He healed people,
arranged for them to be fed, and taught them that God cared for their
well-being, contrary to what might be supposed from the conditions
of their lives. He intentionally violated the social orders that sprang
from the temple as their foundation. He thus called into question the
cult system in which purity, wholeness, forgiveness, and reconsti-
tution were necessarily tied to the temple and its cultic practitioners.[3]

Jesus also favored the views of the Pharisees on the importance of
keeping the laws of Moses, though he is portrayed as rejecting their
supposed social hypocrisy. His purist yet selective approach to the
law is illustrated by his dispute with the Pharisees as portrayed in the
Gospel of Mark. In opposition to the Pharisees' support of divorce
on the authority of Moses, he cited texts from Genesis 1 and Genesis
2 that were believed in his day to be "earlier" than the Pharisees' text
and thus more authoritative.[4]

Jesus' political ambitions are obscure, but it is clear that he headed
a following large and effective enough to be such a threat to both the

3. For a thorough treatment of the priestly purity laws in the New Testament, see L. William
Countryman, *Dirt, Greed, and Sex: Sexual Ethics in the New Testament and Their Implications for
Today* (Philadelphia: Fortress Press, 1988).
4. This is the only quotation from Genesis 1 attributed to Jesus.

Roman occupation and temple authorities that they had him condemned and executed. One recent historian has suggested that as a carpenter he functioned in wider circles than most villagers and served as a broker of relations between groups that otherwise would not get together to deal with their mutual degradation and their ability to aid one another.[5] He thus became a political force to be reckoned with. After his death, his place in the organization he headed was taken by his brother, suggesting the functioning of a family circle with connections and some power. The family organization became established in Jerusalem at the tomb of Jesus in the expectation, not uncommon, that such a powerful individual would reappear in the vicinity of his tomb, conveniently close to the temple as the focus of Judean identity, to carry on his program of social justice for his people.

The Pharisees were preoccupied with belonging to what in their view was the innermost circle of humanity, the people most favored by God. For them, the temple and its cult was the locus of God's interest in people. Belonging to the innermost circle was therefore dependent on one's relation to the temple. This in turn was dependent on observance of the three covenants in the priestly revision of the Torah. Aliens, who observed neither the laws of meat-eating, nor the sign of circumcision, nor the Sabbath, were automatically excluded from the innermost circle, which was reserved for Judeans. The later Jewish scriptures elaborated on the law of Moses and thus paid relatively little attention to the meat law and circumcision.

Like the Pharisees, Jesus focused his attention on the indigenous Judeans of the Palestinian villages and towns. But his concern did not center on belonging to a ritually privileged group, and consequently his attitude toward the covenants was different. Since the covenant of meat-eating encompassed not just the Judeans but all humanity, while the covenant of circumcision included the Ishmaelites, no saying of Jesus is recorded about circumcision and meat-eating. Sayings attributed to him concern only the stipulations of the third covenant, which was limited to Judeans. Jesus' remarks concerning the Sabbath make it clear that he was concerned not with keeping the Sabbath as a way of belonging to a favored group, which is the way the priestly writer presents Sabbath observance, but with whether the Sabbath helped people the way the law of Moses intended it to help them, by giving them rest and relief, and not getting in the way of their restoration. When the keeping of the Sabbath violated the rights of people, then the Sabbath must give way.

Jesus' concern for putting the well-being of individuals ahead of belonging to an inner group through adherence to cultic norms is also evident in the portrayal of his rejection of the bearing of blood on the status of women (Mark 5:21-43). Indeed, it is possible that he rejected entirely the priestly taboo on women and the disabilities that stemmed from that taboo.

PAUL

Although Jesus' acts and teachings are related in the four Gospels, the earliest Christian literature consists of the letters of Paul. Twice Paul alludes to Christ as the means of a new creation in terminology borrowed from Genesis 1:

> It is the God who said, *"Let light shine out of darkness,"* who has shone in our hearts to give the light of the knowledge of the glory of God in the face of Christ. (2 Cor. 4:6, RSV)

> Those he foreknew he also predestined to be conformed to the *image* [Gen. 1:26–27] of his son, in order that he might be the first-born among the brothers. (Rom. 8:29, RSV)

At the beginning of Romans, Paul, like Jesus, appeals to Genesis 1 to argue that because the first reference to human beings as God's creatures stresses that they were male and female, this is the basic order. Hence in describing the disorder that arises in human society when we creatures dishonor the creator, he makes the violation of the category distinction male/female a root of all disorder. In Paul's view, the violation of this order brought on the famous wrath of God against the Sodomites. From such behavior, he asserts, stem all the evils of injustice, greed, malice, murder, deceit, and the rest. Although he does not quote Genesis 1:27, he certainly alludes to it:

> For the wrath of God is revealed from heaven against all impiety and injustice of humans who by their injustice suppress the truth. . . . *Ever since the creation of the world his power and divinity have been clearly perceived in the things that have been made.* . . . Therefore God gave them up in the lusts of their hearts to the impurity

of dishonoring their bodies among themselves, because they exchanged the truth about God for a lie. . . . For this reason God
gave them up to dishonorable passions. Their women exchanged
natural relations for unnatural, and the men likewise gave up natural
relations with women and were consumed with passion for one
another. (RSV, slightly altered)

The fourth and final reference to Genesis 1 in Paul occurs in 1
Corinthians 11:7, where in order to gag women he argues that being
created "in the image of God" refers only to men, not women. There
seems little room for doubt that Paul shared the priestly bias against
women, if not with the same rationale as the priestly taboo.

The main significance for Paul of Genesis 1, however, is again the
issue of inclusion, which for him focused on the question of circumcision, the sign of the second priestly covenant, which embraced not
only Israel but also the Idumeans (Edomites) and, through Ishmael,
the bedouin tribes of the southern deserts. The foremost engagement
with this issue occurs in Galatians. Here Paul refers first to the matter
of food laws, or meat taboos, as defined by the covenant of Moses.
There was ambiguity among Palestinian Judeans on whether the laws
of the covenant of Moses necessarily applied to followers of Christ.
Later the Gospels made an unambiguous point that they did not, but
in the 50s and 60s C.E., before the fall of the temple, there was less
clarity:

> I had been entrusted with the gospel to the uncircumcised, just as
> Peter had been entrusted with the gospel to the circumcised. . . .
> But when Cephas [Peter] came to Antioch I opposed him to his
> face, because he stood condemned. For before certain men came
> from James [Jesus's brother, head of the church in Jerusalem, the
> center for churches' policy], he ate with the aliens [he allowed
> himself to violate the Mosaic meat and blood taboos]. But when
> they came he drew back and separated himself, fearing the circum-
> cision party [those who insisted that the covenant with Abraham
> in P had to be maintained]. (Gal. 2:7, 11-12)

Peter, according to Paul, was eager to press the inclusiveness of
Christian identity beyond the circle of the covenant of Moses, as long
as he did not feel threatened by the other powerful leaders in Jerusalem.
When he did feel threatened, he moved his line of defense back, from
holding to circumcision to holding to the meat laws as well. Paul did

not fault Peter so much for the level of his inclusiveness as for his insincere kowtowing before the hierarchical authority of the church leaders in Jerusalem. His fear of their authority is the proof of the falsehood of his behavior and views. "They make much of you," Paul says regarding church leaders from Jerusalem in a key text in Galatians, "but for no good purpose; they want to shut you out [of inclusion within the covenant people of Christ], that you may make much of them" (Gal. 4:17). The purpose of food laws and circumcision, in Paul's view, was to exclude people so as falsely to bolster the status of others. This was indeed a function of the priestly covenants based on Genesis 1. Paul, living in a different world, rejects it, in theory, out of hand.

In describing his return to Jerusalem (Gal. 2:1-10), Paul explains that his mission to the aliens was condoned in Jerusalem on condition he "remember the poor"—probably the church in Palestine itself—"which very thing I was eager to do." Acts 15 provides a second account of this meeting, written some thirty years later. According to Acts, the issue of inclusion was settled more exactly in terms of the priestly covenants. James's judgment ran as follows:

> My judgment is that we should not trouble those of the aliens who turn to God, but should write to them to abstain from the pollutions of idols and from unchastity and from what is strangled and from blood. For from early generations Moses has had in every city those who preach him, for he is read every Sabbath in the synagogues. (Acts 15:19-21)

These are not miscellaneous taboos that were being imposed on the aliens, but precise rules based on the covenant of Noah. Blood derives explicitly from the covenant of Noah. Strangled meat is likewise meat not drained of blood. Pollutions of idols refers to meat not correctly slaughtered in the priestly manner, hence not in fulfillment of the Mosaic way of keeping the stipulation of the covenant of Noah. Unchastity is based on the same argument that Paul raised in Romans 1, that males should not have sex with males because God created humans male and female, and the son or grandson of Noah was cursed for seeing Noah naked, a curse that led directly to the homosexuality and punishment of the Sodomites. In other words, the inclusion of aliens in the covenant of Christ is governed not by whim but by a strict reading of the priestly Torah. The covenants of Abraham and

Moses do not apply, since the aliens Paul is preaching to fall outside
their descendants; but the covenant of Noah does apply, since everyone
is a child of Noah. And everyone interested in Christ knew about
Noah, because they could hear about him when Moses (that is, the
Torah) was read in synagogue or group-house on the Sabbath, where
Christians could be assumed to assemble.

It is not clear that Acts reports accurately what was decided in
Jerusalem during that momentous meeting. Its reflection of the issue,
though, is probably accurate: the inclusion of the aliens had to be
rationalized in terms of temple scripture. While Paul was relatively
indifferent to the stipulations of the covenant of Moses[6] and argued
vigorously for the suspension of the law of circumcision, he would
have argued equally vigorously for the keeping of the law forbidding
the eating of blood. For him the covenants of the priestly scriptures
still defined who was included among the people of God, and hence
who was included in the covenant of Christ.

MARK

All four Gospels were written after the fall of the temple, and Jesus'
relation to the priestly scriptures is seen in the light of this event. His
relation to these scriptures is also seen in the light of the influence of
alien, non-Judean church leaders, whose concern was with making
the fall of the temple of permanent value for followers of Christ.

The earliest Gospel, Mark, makes the fall of the temple central to
the meaning of Jesus as the Christ. Jesus' three visits to the temple
in Mark 11:11—13:37 constitute an elaborate condemnation of the
temple. His final discourse is a vision of the fall of the temple:

> Do you see these great buildings? There will not be left here one
> stone upon another, that will not be thrown down. . . . From the
> fig tree learn its lesson: as soon as its branch becomes tender and
> puts forth its leaves, you know that *summer* is near.

With the word "summer" the Gospel writer alludes to Amos's vision
in which a basket of summer fruit (Hebrew *qets*) signified the end
(also Hebrew *qets*) of the state and its temple (Amos 8:1-2; also Ezek.
7:5). The temple is, as Jeremiah intimated, no more fruitful than a
barren fig tree. Its purification system is thus discredited:

> Do not trust in these deceptive words: "This is the temple of the
> Lord, the temple of the Lord, the temple of the Lord." . . . Has

---

6. Except when, as in the incident involving Peter, they exposed a lack of sincerity.

this house, which is called by my name, become a den of thieves
in your eyes? Indeed, I myself have seen it, says the Lord. . . .
When I would gather them, says the Lord,

> there are no grapes on the vine,
>   nor figs on the fig tree;
> even the leaves are withered. (Jer. 7:4, 11; 8:13)

In language borrowed from Jeremiah, Mark's Jesus similarly dis-
credits the temple ritual:

> He entered Jerusalem and went into the temple . . . and as it was
> already late, he went out to Bethany.
> The following day, when they came from Bethany [to the
> temple], he was hungry. Seeing in the distance a fig tree in leaf, he
> went to see whether he could find anything on it. When he came
> to it, he found nothing but leaves, for it was not the season for
> figs. And he said, "May no one ever eat fruit from you again." . . .
> And he entered the temple and began to drive out those who sold
> and those who bought in the temple. . . . And he taught them, "Is
> it not written, 'My house shall be called a house of prayer for all
> peoples'? But you have made it a den of thieves." . . . When evening
> came they went out of the city.
> As they passed by in the morning [on their way to the temple],
> they saw the fig tree withered away to its roots. Peter remembered
> and said to him, "Rabbi, look! The fig tree which you cursed has
> withered." Jesus answered them, "Have the faith of God. Truly I
> say to you, whoever says to this mountain, 'Be taken up and thrown
> into the sea,' and does not doubt in their heart, but believes that
> what they say will come to pass, it will be done for them. Therefore
> I tell you, whatever you ask in prayer, believe that you receive it,
> and you will. And whenever you stand praying, forgive, if you
> have anything against any one; so that your father also who is in
> heaven may forgive you your trespasses." (Mark 11:11-25, abbre-
> viated)

The expression "this mountain" refers not to just any mountain but
to the mountain they were looking at, the mountain on which the
temple stood. A person who prayed for this mountain to be thrown
into the sea would be adverting to the original creation account of
the construction of the temple following the subduing of the cosmic
sea. The temple, in Jesus' words, belongs back where it came from,
in the sea of chaos that preceded creation. The destruction of the

temple in Mark's view is the key requirement for the bringing in of nothing less than a new creation, the creation of a new social order—a view already anticipated by Paul.

Without the temple, there could be no rites of settlement (RSV "atonement"), the basis or mark of forgiveness in the view of both the priestly formulators of the temple sacrificial rite and the priests in the time of Jesus.[7] Instead, forgiveness is offered by God, with one human being forgiving another. Such simple forgiveness makes the Herodian, Sadducean temple and its elaborate cult and purification system unnecessary.

Anticipating this revolutionary overthrow of the centrality of the temple, Mark positions a story of Jesus both forgiving and healing a disabled individual early in the Gospel. Four men brought a paralytic to Jesus on a pallet. When they arrived at his house, the crowd of people was so great that they had to tear away some of the roof and let down the pallet through the cavity:

> When Jesus saw their faith, he said to the paralytic, "My son, your sins are forgiven." Now some of the scribes were sitting there, wondering, "Why does this man speak thus? It is blasphemy. Who can forgive sins but God alone?" . . . Jesus said to them, "Which is easier, to say to the paralytic, 'Your sins are forgiven,' or to say, 'Rise, take up your pallet and walk'? But that you may know that this person has the authority on earth to forgive sins"—he said to the paralytic, "I say to you, rise, take up your pallet and go home." (Mark 2:5-11, RSV, slightly altered)

In the view of post-70 C.E. Christians, Jesus claimed that he himself, as a human being, would take the place of the temple and its rites of settlement. The ironies of Mark's narrative of Jesus' trial highlight the witnesses' incredulity and incomprehension at such a revolutionary claim:

> Some stood up and bore false witness against him, saying, "We heard him say, 'I will destroy this temple that is made with hands, and in three days I will build another, not made with hands.' " Yet not even so did their testimony agree. . . . Those who passed by derided him, wagging their heads and saying, "Aha! You who would

---

7. Herbert C. Brichto, "On Slaughter and Sacrifice, Blood and Atonement," *Hebrew Union College Annual* 47 (1976): 35–36.

destroy the temple and build it in three days, save yourself, and come down from the cross." (Mark 14:57-59; 15:29-30, RSV)

In Mark's narrative, the judgment passed on Jesus by the temple authorities turns back on the temple at the instant of his death:

Jesus uttered a loud cry and breathed his last, and the curtain of the temple was torn in two, from top to bottom. (15:37-38, RSV)

Mark may have been written in Palestine or Syria, where for a brief time after 70 C.E. the possibility remained open for Christian communities to sustain themselves. This expectation was shortly to prove mistaken, and by the second century the church had largely disappeared from Palestine, with the exception of Caesarea, the Roman imperial capital in Palestine. Mark deals with the Sabbath, food laws, and blood taboos of the covenant of Moses, but leaves the issue of circumcision aside. His readers assumed the validity of circumcision and the covenant of Abraham. For them the point at issue was the status of the rules of the covenant of Moses. He apparently wrote for readers who recently believed strongly in the authority of James and Peter in Jerusalem, but who had been shocked and become nonplused by the fall of the temple and the discredit that fell as a result on the Jerusalem church and its leaders.

Mark makes the Sabbath the main issue of his entire first set of stories of healing and teaching (1:21—3:6). This section begins: "And they went into Capernaum; and immediately on the Sabbath he entered the synagogue and taught." It concludes: "The Sabbath was made for people, not people for the Sabbath; so this person is lord even of the Sabbath. . . . Is it lawful on the Sabbath to do good or to do harm, to save life or to kill?" The final words of this section look forward to Jesus' trial and execution: "The Pharisees went out, and immediately held counsel with the Herodians against him, how to destroy him."

Mark reports Jesus' teaching on the food laws in the center of his narrative:

"Do you not see that whatever goes into a person from outside cannot defile them, since it enters, not their heart but their stomach, and so passes on?" Thus he declared all foods clean. (Mark 7:18-19)

MATTHEW

Matthew continues the emphasis of Mark on what in the law of Moses
is invalid, but has a more precise view of what is valid and how it is
valid:

> Think not that I have come to abolish the law and the prophets; I
> have come not to abolish them but to fulfill them.

Many laws are to be taken a step further:

> The scribes and Pharisees sit on Moses' seat; so practice and observe
> whatever they tell you, but not what they do; for they preach, but
> do not practice.

Jesus' purpose, in Matthew's view, was to overthrow the temple
and the privileges of those who continued to identify with it, but not
to overthrow the scriptures, the law of Moses. The Pharisees were
the main group whose local view of the scriptures survived, so the
Gospel tends to ascribe to them all the views it opposes, including
the view that the restoration of the temple was to be desired. It even
charges them with the murder of Jesus.

For Matthew it is essential to distinguish between the priestly law
with the temple at its center and the priestly law without a temple.
There are many beneficial laws in the covenant of Moses not contingent on the endurance of the temple. It is these that in Matthew
continue to be enjoined on the Christian, in unprecedentedly strict
terms. Matthew's Jesus lays out the new temple-less law in five dis-
courses that parallel the five scrolls of the temple-based law of Moses.
The prayer of Jesus, from a pre-70 C.E. source, illustrates the validity
of the reinterpreted priestly law as seen by Christians: "Forgive us
our debts as we also have forgiven our debtors." Since the temple no
longer controlled debt and land tenure arrangements, as it had done,
the church as the new society took these into its own hand and
demonstrated how they are to work in God's new creation. Forgiveness of sins extends to the forgiveness of debt between parties in the
newly created templeless society (Mark 11:20-25).

LUKE-ACTS

Like Matthew, Luke is not opposed to the priestly creation-based law
per se, only to its focus on the temple and the social order sanctioned
and controlled by the temple. As for the prophet Micah, for Luke

the fall of the temple requires a reordering of debt and land tenure to the benefit of the poor. Luke–Acts therefore launches Jesus' career with a proclamation of the jubilee-like year of remission:

> He came to Nazareth . . . and went to the synagogue, as his custom was, on the Sabbath day. And he stood up to read, and there was given to him the scroll of the prophet Isaiah. He opened the scroll and found the place where it is written,
>
> > "The spirit of Yahweh is upon me, because he has anointed me to preach good news to the poor. He has sent me to proclaim release to the captives and recovering of sight to the blind, to set at *liberty* those who are oppressed, to proclaim the year of Yahweh's favor of the poor."
>
> And he closed the scroll, and gave it back to the attendant, and sat down . . . and began to say to them, "Today this scripture has been fulfilled in your hearing." (Luke 4:16-21, RSV)

The liberty of the jubilee remission announced here produces benefits for the poor and not for the temple. This is in contrast to the priestly writer and Third Isaiah, who viewed the jubilee as a way of benefiting the poor and the temple together. The priestly writer and Third Isaiah accepted as valid the premise that the poor received benefit from the temple. The Christian gospel adopted in the post-70 C.E. period rejected this premise.

The priestly writer and Third Isaiah also assumed that, even though God's justice expressed through the temple was the ultimate justice, the rule of Persia in Palestine could assist the poor with justice. Luke did not discard this assumption that the empire's rule in Palestine could bring justice. It is noteworthy that the empire's role in Jesus' death is muted in the Gospel. Luke, furthermore, makes explicit the substitution of Roman rule for Persian rule: the entire final third of Acts shows Paul seeking justice in Rome. In actual fact, Paul probably lost his case in Rome. It is remarkable that, although Acts was written well after this outcome would have become known, its narrative concludes before Paul's case is resolved, suggesting that Luke did not want to undermine the premise that Rome's justice was an acceptable substitute for the temple's.

The narrative of Luke–Acts commences with a lengthy section elaborating Jesus' relationship with the doomed institution of the temple. Luke's Jesus denounces the temple in the same terms as does

Mark's, and is murdered for it. Stephen exegetes the Torah and proves that the temple is never referred to there, and is murdered for it. The narrative ends with Paul's appeal to the jurisdiction of Rome against the Judean rulers attached to the temple, who have attempted to murder him. In the view of Luke-Acts, the temple and those who continue to be attached to it are opposed to the life of the poor, who are released from bondage with Jesus and whose economic advancement is the proof of God's justice.

It is Luke who, using the categories of the priestly writer, in Acts 15 makes exact the terms of inclusion in the Christian community. In Luke's view, which is consistent with the Torah's account of the Exodus and with the prophets in scripture, the poor define the character of God's favored people. The circle within which God's justice operates, as defined by the life of the poor, was in Luke's view ideally the same circle defined by the Torah of Moses as the keeping of the stipulations of the covenant of Noah.

JOHN

Although John is a distinctive Gospel, here also the followers of Jesus are distinguished from "Judeans" primarily on the basis of their relationship to the temple. John begins with the famous allusion to God's creative word that speaks creation into being in Genesis 1: "In the beginning was the word." This word, embodied in Jesus and the judgment he brings, is what both exposes the injustice of the temple-centered creation and re-creates a world of just judgment. The creation is valid, and its validity requires reiteration. God does not reside among his people in a temple, but instead "tabernacles" with them:

> The word became a living being and tabernacled among us, full of constancy and truth; we have beheld his status. (John 1:14)

In the Gospel of John, God continues to be present with humanity by the same spirit that moved upon the waters in Genesis and by which the first tabernacle was constructed. As in the other Gospels, Jesus foretells the destruction of the temple, then himself embodies the new temple. As Jacob at Bethel saw the angels of God ascending and descending on a giant stairway into heaven and recognized the place he was in as the locus of God's presence among humans, so Jesus pictured himself as a new *beth-ʾel*—a new "temple of God":

> You will see heaven opened, and the angels of God ascending and descending upon this human being. (John 1:51)

Unlike Matthew, Mark, and Luke, in which Jesus visits the temple only at the end of his ministry, in John's Gospel Jesus makes three visits to the temple which are spread out to span the Gospel. Upon his first visit to the temple:

> He found those who were selling oxen and sheep and pigeons [for sacrifice], and the money-changers at their business. Making a whip of cords, he drove them all, with the sheep and oxen, out of the temple. He poured out the coins of the money-changers and over-turned their tables. He told those who sold the pigeons [to the poorest worshipers], "Take these things away; you shall not make my father's house a house of trade." His disciples remembered that it was written, "Zeal for your house will consume me." The Judeans then said to him, "What sign have you to show us for doing this?" Jesus answered them, "Destroy this temple, and in three days I will raise it up." The Judeans then said, "It has taken forty-six years to build this temple, and will you raise it up in three days?" But he spoke of the temple of his body. (John 2:14-21)

Before long Jesus was instructing a Samaritan woman regarding the locality of true worship:

> Woman, believe me, the hour is coming when neither on this moun-tain nor in Jerusalem will you worship the father. . . . The hour is coming and now is when the true worshipers will worship the father in spirit and truth, for such the father seeks to worship him. God is spirit, and those who worship him must worship in spirit and truth. (John 4:21-24)

As is made clear later in the Gospel, the expression "spirit and truth" pertains to fair and honest judgment, the basis of true justice in society.

In John's view, the laws of Moses are valid but require reform in view of the transience of the temple:

> The law was given through Moses; grace and truth [that is, justice in the application of the law] came through Jesus Christ. . . . Do not think that I shall accuse you to the father; it is Moses who accuses you, on whom you have set your hope. If you believed Moses, you would believe me, for he wrote of me. But if you do not believe his writings, how will you believe my words? (John 1:17; 5:45-47, RSV)

If Moses is valid, then the stipulations of the covenants of Moses and Abraham as defined in the context of the temple cult are not.

Jesus therefore carries on a lengthy debate with the Pharisees on the legitimacy of their claim to be sons of Abraham, a reference to their circumcision (John 8:1-59). Jesus ends by asserting, "Before Abraham was, I am." His claim that his word took precedence over the temple as the vehicle of the spirit in re-creating order and justice, coupled with the hardly veiled blasphemy of calling himself the "I am," provoked the Pharisees to take up "stones to throw at him; but Jesus hid himself, and went out of the temple."

HEBREWS

In the period following the fall of the temple, the most elaborate commentary dealing explicitly with the significance of the priestly rites based on Genesis 1 was written by the author of Hebrews. For this author, faith has to do with what is invisible, as proven in creation itself: "By faith we understand that the world was created by the word of God, so that what is seen was made out of things which do not appear" (Heb. 11:3). In this New Testament letter, the priestly cult is subjected to a detailed quasi-Platonist critique and judged to fall short of the standard of invisibility. Everything described by the priestly writer is compromised by its substantiality. Behind it all there is another, invisible, meaning, which is that the high priest is actually, invisibly, Jesus Christ, and the sacrifice is his own.

Hebrews was more than a Platonist critique, however. The trial epitomized by the exodus, still the centerpiece of the priestly Torah, had again to be endured. In Hebrew culture, as the writer of Hebrews knew, faith is not just the confidence of the wrongly accused, but the truth of witnesses for them and of testimony in their favor. The description of faith in Hebrews 11 is permeated with the language of the legal court: faith is the "substantiation" (RSV: "assurance") and "proof" (RSV: "conviction") that provided the "true witness" (RSV: "received divine approval") for the righteous elders of the Hebrew scriptures and does so again for believers in the post-70 C.E. era. What was created by faith was what was hoped for but not yet seen: the vindication, justification, and acquittal of those wrongly accused and punished. The adjudication that accompanied the cult was thus relocated in Christ, in whom the ineffectual and false substantiation of the temple's cult was suspended.

The theory implicit in earlier Christian writers and articulated in Hebrews accomplished the final dissolution of any bond between Christians and the priestly interpretation of the scriptures. The sacerdotal character of Christian faith and practice was thereby left to be built anew within three centuries under the jurisdictional favor of Rome.

Epilogue:
Creation in Our Time

The priestly writers inhabited a strange and fascinating world. We think of the priests as the religious heads of the nation, yet most of what they did involved caring for their expensive paraphernalia and butchering animals. They supervised the writing of texts that were practically secret texts. They thought of the temple as a tent, an act of imagining the world as other than it actually is. At the same time as they were the beneficiaries of the people's hard work, they sanctioned laws meant to ameliorate the people's distress.

The priests of Jerusalem formed a virtual caste. The privileges of a few fortunate males of high rank are unexpressed but no less present in the priestly account of creation, which like all accounts of creation in the ancient world reflects the social reality that feeds it. This elite fraternity represented the prime practitioners in Judah of the ancient creed of the religious specialist: rite makes right.

CONTACTS WITH OUR WORLD

The priests of the sixth century B.C.E. did not design their rite to appeal to the instincts of those of us who are at home in the industrialized world of the twentieth century. Modern urban sensibilities may find it difficult to abide the odor of still warm blood and reeking offal; the bleating, squawking, and barking of excited animals; and the clanging and scraping of slaughterhouse paraphernalia that float

in and out between the august lines of Genesis 1. Beyond anthropological curiosity, the temptation may lie close at hand to regard the
creation story of Genesis 1 as nonsense.

Yet the priestly world makes intriguing contacts with our own.
These go well beyond the inordinate consumption of meat in America,
to say nothing of the rite of the communal barbecue. With surprisingly
little translation, the priestly world is our world. To the priestly
writers, creation had to do with realities like food, birth, and land
tenure. In the priestly concept, these basics of social life properly
found their meaning in relation to worship. So it is with us, even if
time and money—the elements of the capitalist order—take the place
of land, grain, and livestock, the elements of the agrarian order. The
priestly concept of creation conveyed a broad sense of integration and
comprehensiveness. Everything of importance was interrelated. The
priests' creative speculation gave exquisite expression to this primary
religious impulse: holiness, as a function of the interrelatedness of all
essentials, transforms the ordinary into sacred signs of God's creation.

The same kind of speculation, then as now, promoted another,
contrary religious impulse—one with which we are also familiar.
Order and structure in any society seem to require that there be a
hierarchy that functions as a center for the nation, with the bulk of
the people at its periphery. This hierarchy defined those who were in
and those who were out. Thus holiness, as defined by such a hierarchy,
also tends to relegate the ordinary—everyday people and the neces-
sities of life—to the bottom, the periphery, the outside. This costs the
lives of the poor. In a word, blood, the sign of the creation of life,
is shed. In the priests' order, to acknowledge life was to destroy life.
This destruction of life included, quite against the priests' intent, the
severe diminution of the life of ordinary people.

Such a contradiction was not the monopoly of the ancient Jerusalem
priesthood. Indeed, the sort of theorizing done by the priests to rationalize their ordered life in the midst of what is in fact a disordered
and disorderly society typically provides the basis of privilege that is
a succor to one person but life-threatening or life-destroying to another. It defines such privilege, and it confirms such privilege. The
primary privilege is that which the priests arrogated to themselves,
of conceiving, implementing, and benefiting from the distinction between the holy and the common. This is the privilege that all sacred
rites foster, and that all persons assume who presume to put people,

goods, and activities in classes and categories. This is the privilege that undergirded the rank of priest. This is the privilege that, in the words of the priestly Psalm 8, placed its beneficiaries in the rank of the divine ("you have made him little less than God"). The making of distinctions, in imitation of God's creation by division and demarcation, undergirds the distinction of the priesthood, and the separation of the priesthood from what is common. All social groups follow the lead of Jerusalem's ancient priests and engage in such demarcation and confirm it with theorizing and ideology.

STRUCTURED PRIVILEGE: REFORM AND REVOLUTION

Whether the awareness of this propensity to support privilege with rationalization can mitigate its contribution to social disorder is an open question. Privilege is no more intrinsically evil than is separatism. The justification of privilege naturally varies according to its historical function. The privilege of demarcated social identity may not only oppress, but also redeem, at least in the interim. Which it does depends on the historical context. Throughout history, oppressed groups have formed demarcated organizations in which to conceive of themselves as the righteous, and on the basis of this conception to work for their own deliverance from oppression.

There exist two common ways to conceive of the redemptive quality of structured privilege. These are really two ways to conceive of the practice of justice. According to the first, privilege confers responsibility. In the words of De Levis, spoken on the threshold of the modern order, "Nobility obligates." The privileged use their position to maintain or restore good order. This is the reformist approach.

According to the second, revolutionary approach, opposing orders invariably conflict, and with God's help the good order overcomes the bad. The oppressed fight fire with fire, adopting the privilege of order in defense. In the resulting struggle, the right wins out. The privilege bestowed by revolutionary order overthrows the privilege cemented by oppressive social order.

Which of two privileges, based on two definitions of order, is right—and thus which of two conflicting rites is right—hinges on the history of the groups involved, not on the intrinsic nature of privilege based on social order. Both these approaches, of responsibility and conflict, reform and revolution, play an ongoing role in history. Wealth and poverty are perhaps the commonest standard, though not the only one, by which to judge an order's rectitude.

Both approaches are found in the Bible. Reform movements find expression in the great texts that accompanied the change from one established government to another: David's J, Jeroboam's E, Josiah's Deuteronomistic work, the priestly history, Ezra, and Nehemiah. These define order mainly in terms of history and law. Revolutionary movements find their expression in the concept of a new creation. In the Bible, new creation is as important as creation. New creation finds its quintessential expression in the great texts of prophecy: Amos, Isaiah, Jeremiah, Ezekiel, Zechariah, and others. These define order mainly in terms of the judgment of God, which cannot be predicted and may equally result in mercy as in wrath. Mercy, the precious opening for the oppressed, violated, ousted, and abused, violates the established order. Such violation is difficult to express in the rigidities of structure and defined order, and hence its metaphors tend to be organic, as with a new birth.

The priestly writing appears to deal more with reform than new creation, yet it holds to both. As seen in chapter 11, it obviously presents a reform program. It also conceives of a new creation, recognizable for example in its tacit concept of the re-creation of the temple as a tent, or its near exclusion of the monarchy from a defined national role. The priestly writing embodies this dual concept not least because in its present form it stems from the experience of profound disenfranchisement. In other words, its starting point is not just the traditions of the established priesthood of monarchic Jerusalem, but also the real collapse of created order as the priests of Jerusalem knew it.

Here lie the priestly writing's ties with both its Christian and Jewish scriptural descendants. Both the New Testament and the Mishnah, as bodies of scripture rooted in the Hebrew scriptures, were ultimately founded in the chaos and disorder of the fall of the temple in 70 C.E. The early church's reformist commitment to Roman jurisdiction, and the early rabbis' commitment to renewed local jurisdiction, along with the conception among both groups of the new creation of new orders (such as the validation of "oral law"), arose out of that catastrophe. For neither group and its scriptures could the ancient priestly rite as such, or its privileges, any longer hold their validity (even though priestly families persisted among Judeans under rabbinic jurisdiction).

CHOICE OF ORDERS

Thus the choice every religious person and group faces is not between order and nonorder in their lives, but between one order and another. The sacerdotal task is to conceptualize and propose actions that point to the order of creation that incorporates the possibility of new creation.

God's spirit is the creative, revolutionary spirit. No later than the beginning of time, at the inception of the priestly history, the spirit of God hovered over the ubiquitous, shapeless waters, in the darkness, pregnant with the form of creation. Throughout the scriptures of the priesthood, this spirit creates new orders where disorder prevails, as in the priestly account of the creation of the order governing the disposition of lifeblood and the corresponding creation of the crafted tabernacle (Exod. 31:3; 35:31), or of the Christian evangelist's account of rebirth in judgment (John 3), or the apostle's of his encounter with spirited women (1 Corinthians), or of the Jewish sage's reinterpretation of law. The spirit bestowed on Bezalel "ability, intelligence, knowledge, and all craft"—that is, the miraculous discipline of his artistry. On others it bestows the license of a new order. The true spirit of creation is thus the spirit of order and discipline in a new creation.

Both Jews and Christians speak therefore of spiritual disciplines, the prophetic practices of the new order that is emerging out of the disorder with which we are too familiar. In the end as in the beginning, it is such practices and their spirit that prefigure God's born-again creation.

For Further Reading

INTRODUCTION

Berra, Tim M. *Evolution and the Myth of Creationism: A Basic Guide to the Facts in the Evolution Debate,* Stanford: Stanford University Press, 1990.

Carvin, W. P. *Creation and Scientific Explanation.* Edinburgh: Scottish Academic Press, 1988.

Hyers, Conrad. *The Meaning of Creation: Genesis and Modern Science.* Atlanta: John Knox Press, 1984.

Livingstone, David N. *Darwin's Forgotten Defenders: The Encounter Between Evangelical Theology and Evolutionary Thought.* Grand Rapids: Eerdmans, 1987.

Marsden, George. "A Case of the Excluded Middle: Creation Versus Evolution in America." In *Uncivil Religion,* ed. Robert Bellah and Frederick Greenspahn. New York: Crossroad, 1987, 132–55.

Ruse, Michael, ed. *But Is It Science? The Philosophical Question in the Creation/Evolution Controversy.* Buffalo: Prometheus Books, 1988.

Van Till, Howard J., ed. *Portraits of Creation: Biblical and Scientific Perspectives on the World's Formation.* Grand Rapids: Eerdmans, 1990.

Wills, Garry. *Under God: Religion and American Politics.* New York: Simon and Schuster, 1990, 97–124.

Young, Davis A. *Christianity and the Age of the Earth.* Grand Rapids: Zondervan, 1982.

CHAPTER ONE

Brandon, S. G. F. *Creation Legends of the Ancient Near East.* London: Hodder & Stoughton, 1963.

Clifford, Richard J. "Cosmogonies in the Ugaritic Texts and in the Bible." *Orientalia* 53 (1984): 183–201.

Coogan, Michael David. *Stories from Ancient Canaan.* Philadelphia: Westminster, 1978.

Doria, Charles, and Harris Lenowitz, eds. *Creation Texts from the Ancient Mediterranean.* Garden City: Doubleday, 1975.

Fisher, Loren R. "Creation at Ugarit and in the Old Testament." *Vetus Testamentum* 15 (1965): 313–24.

Frymer-Kensky, Tikva. "The Planting of Man: A Study in Biblical Imagery." In *Love and Death in the Ancient Near East: Essays in Honor of Marvin H. Pope,* ed. John H. Marks and Robert M. Good. Guilford, Conn.: Four Quarters Publishing Company, 1987, 129–36.

Heidel, Alexander. *The Babylonian Genesis: The Story of Creation.* Chicago: University of Chicago Press, 1942[1], 1951[2].

Jacobsen, Thorkild. "The Eridu Genesis." *Journal of Biblical Literature* 100 (1981): 513–29.

Koch, Klaus. "Wort und Einheit des Schöpfergottes in Memphis und Jerusalem." *Zeitschrift für Theologie und Kirche* 62 (1965): 251–93.

Menu, Bernadette. "Les cosmogonies de l'ancienne Egypte." In *La création dans l'Orient Ancien.* Congress of the Association catholique française pour l'étude de la Bible, Lille, 1985, ed. Fabien Blanquart. Paris: Editions du Cerf, 1987, 97–120.

Müller, Hans Peter. "Eine neue babylonische Menschenschöpfungserzählung im Licht keilschriftlicher und biblischer Parallelen." *Orientalia* 58 (1989): 61–85.

Oppenheim, A. Leo. *Ancient Mesopotamia: Portrait of a Dead Civilization.* Chicago: University of Chicago Press, 1964, 183–98, "The Care and Feeding of the Gods."

Pritchard, James B., ed. *Ancient Near Eastern Texts Relating to the Old Testament.* 2d ed. Princeton: Princeton University Press, 1955.

Seux, Marie-Joseph. "La création du monde et de l'homme dans la littérature suméro-akkadienne." In *La création dans l'Orient Ancien,* Congress of the Association catholique française pour l'étude de la Bible, Lille, 1985, ed. Fabien Blanquart. Paris: Editions du Cerf, 1987, 41–78.

CHAPTER TWO

Anderson, Bernhard W. "Creation." In *The Interpreter's Dictionary of the Bible,* ed. George Arthur Buttrick. Nashville: Abingdon Press, 1962, vol. 1, 725–32.

———, ed. *Creation in the Old Testament.* Issues in Religion and Theology, 6. Philadelphia: Fortress Press, 1984.

Clifford, Richard J. "The Hebrew Scriptures and the Theology of Creation." *Theological Studies* 46 (1985): 507–23.

Fishbane, Michael. "Jeremiah IV 23–26 and Job III 3–13: A Recovered Use of the Creation Pattern." *Vetus Testamentum* 21 (1971): 151–67.

CHAPTER THREE

Beard, Mary, and John North, eds. *Pagan Priests: Religion and Power in the Ancient World.* Ithaca: Cornell University Press, 1990.

Budd, P. J. "Holiness and Cult." In *The World of Ancient Israel: Sociological, Anthropological and Political Perspectives,* ed. R. E. Clements. Cambridge: Cambridge University Press, 1989, 275–98.

Clévenot, Michel. *Materialist Approaches to the Bible.* Maryknoll, N.Y.: Orbis Books, 1985, 35–41, "The Priestly Caste, the P Document, and the System of Purity."

Cody, Aelred. *A History of the Old Testament Priesthood.* Rome: Pontifical Biblical Institute, 1969.

Cross, Frank M. *Canaanite Myth and Hebrew Epic.* Cambridge: Harvard University Press, 1973, 195–215.

Friedman, Richard E. *Who Wrote the Bible?* New York: Summit Books, 1987.

Hallo, William W. "The Origins of the Sacrificial Cult: New Evidence from Mesopotamia and Israel." In *Ancient Israelite Religion: Essays in Honor of Frank Moore Cross,* ed. Patrick D. Miller, Paul D. Hanson, and S. Dean McBride. Philadelphia: Fortress Press, 1987, 3–13.

Haran, Menahem. *Temples and Temple-Service in Ancient Israel: An Inquiry into the Character of Cult Phenomena and the Historical Setting of the Priestly School.* Oxford: Clarendon Press, 1978.

Kautsky, John H. *The Politics of Aristocratic Empires.* Chapel Hill: University of North Carolina Press, 1982.

Lenski, Gerhard E. *Power and Privilege: A Theory of Social Stratification.* New York: McGraw-Hill, 1966; Chapel Hill: University of North Carolina Press, 1984, 256–66.

Levine, Baruch A. "Priests." In *Interpreter's Dictionary of the Bible,* Supplementary Volume, ed. Keith Crim. Nashville: Abingdon Press, 1976, 687–90.

McEwan, Gilbert J. P. "Distribution of Meat in Eanna." *Iraq* 45 (1983): 187–98.

Meyers, Eric M. "The Shelomith Seal and the Judean Restoration: Some Additional Considerations." *Eretz Israel* 18 (1985): 33*–38*.

Rivkin, Ellis. "Aaron, Aaronides." In *Interpreter's Dictionary of the Bible,* Supplementary Volume, ed. Keith Crim. Nashville: Abingdon Press, 1976, 1–3.

Sjoberg, Gideon. *The Preindustrial City, Past and Present.* New York: Free Press, Macmillan, 1960.

Vaux, Roland de. *Ancient Israel.* Vol. 2, *Religious Institutions.* New York: McGraw-Hill, 1961.

Wenham, Gordon J. *The Book of Leviticus.* Grand Rapids: Eerdmans, 1979, 47–160.

CHAPTER FOUR

Beauchamp, Paul. "Création et fondation de la loi en Gn 1, 1–2, 4." In *La création dans l'Orient Ancien.* Congress of the Association catholique française pour l'étude de la Bible, Lille, 1985, ed. Fabien Blanquart. Paris: Editions du Cerf, 1987, 139–82.

Blenkinsopp, Joseph. "The Structure of P." *Catholic Biblical Quarterly* 38 (1976): 275–92.

Brueggemann, Walter. "The Kerygma of the Priestly Writers." In *The Vitality of Old Testament Traditions,* ed. Walter Brueggemann and Hans Walter Wolff. Atlanta: John Knox Press, 1975[1], 1982[2], 101–13.

Cross, Frank Moore. *Canaanite Myth and Hebrew Epic: Essays in the History of the Religion of Israel.* Cambridge: Harvard University Press, 1973, 293–325, "The Priestly Work."

Cryer, F. H. "The Interrelationships of Gen 5, 32; 11, 10–11 and the Chronology of the Flood (Gen 6–9)." *Biblica* 66 (1985): 241–61.

Emerton, J. A. "The Priestly Writer in Genesis." *Journal of Theological Studies* 39 (1988): 381–400.

Fishbane, Michael. *Text and Texture: Close Readings of Selected Biblical Texts*. New York: Schocken Books, 1979, 3–16.

Friedman, Richard E. *The Exile and Biblical Narrative: The Formation of the Deuteronomistic and Priestly Works*. Chico: Scholars Press, 1981, 44–136.

Fritz, Volkmar. "Das Geschichtsverständnis der Priesterschrift." *Zeitschrift für Theologie und Kirche* 84 (1987): 426–39.

Frymer-Kensky, Tikva. "The Atrahasis Epic and Its Significance for Our Understanding of Genesis 1–9." *Biblical Archaeologist* 40 (1977): 147–55.

Gottwald, Norman K. *The Hebrew Bible: A Socio-Literary Introduction*. Philadelphia: Fortress Press, 1985, 469–82.

Habel, Norman C. *Literary Criticism of the Old Testament*. Philadelphia: Fortress Press, 1971.

Renaud, B. "Les généalogies et la structure de l'histoire sacerdotale dans le livre de la Genèse." *Revue biblique* 97 (1990): 5–30.

Saebø, Magne. "Priestertheologie und Priesterschrift: Zur Eigenart der priesterlichen Schicht im Pentateuch." In *Congress Volume: Vienna 1980,* Supplements to *Vetus Testamentum,* 32, ed. J. A. Emerton, Leiden: Brill, 1981, 357–74.

Weimar, P. "Sinai und Schöpfung: Komposition und Theologie der priesterschriftlichen Sinaigeschichte." *Revue biblique* 95 (1988): 337–85.

Zenger, E. *Gottes Bogen in den Wolken: Untersuchungen zu Komposition und Theologie der priesterschriftlichen Urgeschichte*. Stuttgart: Verlag Katholische Bibelwerk, 1983.

CHAPTER FIVE

Bird, Phyllis. " 'Male and Female He Created Them': Genesis 1:27b in the Context of the Priestly Account of Creation." *Harvard Theological Review* 74 (1981): 129–59.

————. "Sexual Differentiation and Divine Image in the Genesis Creation Texts." In *Image of God and Gender Models*, ed. Kari Børresen. Oslo: Solum Forlag, forthcoming.

Steck, Odil Hannes. *Der Schöpfungsbericht der Priesterschrift: Studien zur literarkritischen und überlieferungsgeschichtlichen Problematik von Genesis 1, 1–2, 4a.* Göttingen: Vandenhoeck & Ruprecht, 1975[1], 1981[2].

Weinfeld, Moshe. "Sabbath, Temple and the Enthronement of the Lord: The Problem of the Sitz im Leben of Genesis 1:1—2:3." In *Festschrift Cazelles*, Altes Orient und Altes Testament 212. Neukirchen-Vluyn: Neukirchener Verlag, 1981, 501–11.

CHAPTER SIX

Douglas, Mary. *Purity and Danger: An Analysis of Concepts of Pollution and Taboo.* Harmondsworth: Penguin Books, 1966, 54–72, "The Abominations of Leviticus."

Eilberg-Schwartz, Howard. "Creation and Classification in Judaism: From Priestly to Rabbinic Conceptions." *History of Religions* 26 (1987): 357–81.

Harris, Marvin. *Cows, Pigs, Wars, and Witches: The Riddles of Culture.* New York: Random House, 1974, 28–38, "Pig Lovers and Pig Haters."

————. *Good to Eat: Riddles of Food and Culture.* New York: Simon and Schuster, 1985, 67–87, "The Abominable Pig."

Hesse, Brian. "Animal Use at Tel Miqne-Ekron in the Bronze Age and Iron Age." *Bulletin of the American Schools of Oriental Research* 264 (1986): 17–27.

Hübner, Ulrich. "Schweine, Schweineknochen und ein Speiseverbot im alten Israel." *Vetus Testamentum* 39 (1989): 225–36.

McEwan, Gilbert J. P. "Distribution of Meat in Eanna." *Iraq* 45 (1983): 187–98.

Milgrom, Jacob. "The Biblical Diet Laws as an Ethical System: Food and Faith." *Interpretation* 17 (1963): 288–301. Reprinted in Jacob Milgrom, *Studies in Cultic Theology and Terminology.* Leiden: Brill, 1983, 104–18.

Pond, Wilson G. "Modern Pork Production." *Scientific American* 248:5 (May 1983): 96–103.

Soler, Jean. "The Dietary Prohibitions of the Hebrews." *The New York Review of Books,* June 14, 1979: 24–30 (from *Food and Drink in History,* Baltimore: Johns Hopkins University Press, 1979).

Stachowiak, L. "Der Sinn der sogenannten Noachitischen Gebote (Genesis ix 1–7)." In *Congress Volume: Vienna 1980.* Supplements to *Vetus Testamentum,* 32, ed. J. A. Emerton. Leiden: Brill, 1981, 395–404.

Wenham, Gordon J. *The Book of Leviticus.* Grand Rapids: Eerdmans, 1979, 161–85.

CHAPTER SEVEN

Biale, David. "The God with Breasts: El Shaddai in the Bible." *History of Religions* 21 (1982): 240–56.

Bird, Phyllis A. " 'Male and Female He Created Them': Gen. 1:27b in the Context of the Priestly Account of Creation." *Harvard Theological Review* 74 (1981): 129–59.

———. "The Place of Women in the Israelite Cultus." In *Ancient Israelite Religion: Essays in Honor of Frank Moore Cross,* ed. Patrick D. Miller, Paul D. Hanson, and S. Dean McBride. Philadelphia: Fortress Press, 1987, 397–419.

Gruber, Mayer I. "Women in the Cult According to the Priestly Code." In *Judaic Perspectives on Ancient Israel,* ed. Jacob Neusner. Philadelphia: Fortress Press, 1987, 35–48.

Knauf, Ernst Axel. "El Shaddai—der Gott Abrahams?" *Biblische Zeitschrift* 29 (1985): 97–103.

Paige, Karen Ericksen, and Jeffery M. Paige. *The Politics of Reproductive Ritual*. Berkeley: University of California Press, 1981, 122–66, "Male Circumcision: The Dilemma of Fission."

Weimar, Peter. "Genesis 17 und die priesterschriftliche Abrahamsgeschichte." *Zeitschrift für die alttestamentliche Wissenschaft* 100 (1988): 22–60.

CHAPTER EIGHT

Andreasen, Niels-Erik A. *The Old Testament Sabbath: A Tradition-Historical Investigation*. Missoula: Society of Biblical Literature, 1972.

Colson, F. H. *The Week: An Essay on the Origin and Development of the Seven-Day Cycle*. Cambridge: Cambridge University Press, 1926.

Gaster, Theodor H. *Festivals of the Jewish Year: A Modern Interpretation and Guide*. New York: Morrow, 1952.

Hallo, William W. "New Moons and Sabbaths: A Case-Study in the Contrastive Approach." *Hebrew Union College Annual* 48 (1977): 1–18.

Kearney, Peter J. "Creation and Liturgy: The P Redaction of Ex. 25–40." *Zeitschrift für die alttestamentliche Wissenschaft* 89 (1977): 375–87.

Lemaire, André. "Le sabbat à l'époque royale israélite." *Revue biblique* 80 (1973): 161–85.

Rochberg-Halton, F. "Elements of the Babylonian Contribution to Hellenistic Astrology." *Journal of the American Oriental Society* 108 (1988): 51–62.

Shafer, Byron E. "Sabbath." In *Interpreter's Dictionary of the Bible*, Supplementary Volume, ed. Keith Crim. Nashville: Abingdon Press, 1976, 760–62.

Tigay, Jeffrey H. *"shabbat."* In *Encyclopedia Miqra'it.* Jerusalem: Bialik Institute, 1950–1982, vol. 7, cols. 504–17.

CHAPTER NINE

Clifford, Richard J. "The Tent of El and the Israelite Tent of Meeting." *Catholic Biblical Quarterly* 33 (1971): 221–27.

Cross, Frank M. "The Tabernacle: A Study from an Archaeological and Historical Approach." *Biblical Archaeologist* 10 (1947): 45–68. Revised and reprinted as "The Priestly Tabernacle," in *The Biblical Archaeologist Reader,* ed. G. Ernest Wright and D. N. Freedman. Garden City: Doubleday Anchor Books, 1961, 201–28.

———. "The Priestly Tabernacle in the Light of Recent Research." In *The Temple in Antiquity,* ed. T. G. Madsden. Provo, Utah: Religious Studies Center, Brigham Young University, 1984, 91–105

Fritz, Volkmar. *Tempel und Zelt: Studien zum Tempelbau in Israel und zu dem Zeltheiligtum der Priesterschrift.* Neukirchen: Neukirchener Verlag, 1977.

Hurowitz, Victor. "The Priestly Account of the Building of the Tabernacle." *Journal of the American Oriental Society* 105 (1985): 21–30.

CHAPTER TEN

Anderson, Gary A. *Sacrifice and Offerings in Ancient Israel: Studies in their Social and Political Importance.* Atlanta: Scholars Press, 1987.

Bailey, Lloyd R. *Leviticus.* Knox Preaching Guides. Atlanta: John Knox Press, 1987.

Baker, David W. "Leviticus 1-7 and the Punic Tariffs: A Form Critical Comparison." *Zeitschrift für die alttestamentliche Wissenschaft* 99 (1987): 188–97.

Brichto, Herbert C. "On Slaughter and Sacrifice, Blood and Atonement." *Hebrew Union College Annual* 47 (1976): 19–55.

Davies, Douglas. "An Interpretation of Sacrifice in Leviticus." *Zeitschrift für die alttestamentliche Wissenschaft* 89 (1977): 387–99.

Detienne, Marcel, and Jean-Pierre Vernant, eds. *The Cuisine of Sacrifice Among the Greeks*. Chicago: University of Chicago Press, 1989.

Eilberg-Schwarz, Howard. *The Savage in Judaism: An Anthropology of Israelite Religion and Ancient Judaism*. Bloomington: Indiana University Press, 1990.

Frymer-Kensky, Tikva. "Pollution, Purification, and Purgation in Biblical Israel." In *The Word of the Lord Shall Go Forth: Essays in Honor of David Noel Freedman,* ed. Carol L. Meyers and M. O'Connor. Winona Lake: American Schools of Oriental Research and Eisenbrauns, 1983, 399–414.

Gaster, Theodor H. "Sacrifices and Offerings, OT." In *Interpreter's Dictionary of the Bible,* Supplementary Volume, ed. Keith Crim. Nashville: Abingdon Press, 1976, 147–59.

Geller, M. J. "The Shurpu Incantations and Lev. V. 1–5." *Journal of Semitic Studies* 25 (1980): 181–92.

Gray, George Buchanan. *Sacrifice in the Old Testament: Its Theory and Practice*. 1925 reprint. New York: KTAV, 1971.

Haran, Menahem. *Temples and Temple-Service in Ancient Israel: An Inquiry into the Character of Cult Phenomena and the Historical Setting of the Priestly School*. Oxford: Clarendon Press, 1978.

Hecht, Richard D. "Studies on Sacrifice, 1970–1980." *Religious Studies Review* 8:3 (July 1982): 253–59.

Henninger, Joseph. "Sacrifice." In *The Encyclopedia of Religion,* ed. Mircea Eliade. New York: Macmillan, 1987, vol. 12, 544–57.

Kiuchi, N. *The Purification Offering in the Priestly Literature: Its Meaning and Function*. Sheffield: JSOT Press, 1987.

Levine, Baruch A. *In the Presence of the Lord: A Study of Cult and Some Cultic Terms in Ancient Israel.* Leiden: Brill, 1974.

———. *The JPS Torah Commentary: Leviticus.* Philadelphia: The Jewish Publication Society, 1989.

McCarthy, Dennis J. "The Symbolism of Blood and Sacrifice." *Journal of Biblical Literature* 88 (1969): 166–76.

———. "Further Notes on the Symbolism of Blood and Sacrifice." *Journal of Biblical Literature* 92 (1973): 205–10.

Milgrom, Jacob. *Cult and Conscience: The Asham and the Priestly Doctrine of Repentance.* Leiden: Brill, 1976.

———. "The Cultic *šggh* and Its Influence in Psalms and Job." *Jewish Quarterly Review* 58 (1967): 115–25.

———. "Leviticus." In *Interpreter's Dictionary of the Bible,* Supplementary Volume, ed. Keith Crim. Nashville: Abingdon Press, 1976, 541–45.

———. "A Prolegomenon to Leviticus 17:11." *Journal of Biblical Literature* 90 (1971): 149–56.

———. "Sacrifices and Offerings, OT." In *Interpreter's Dictionary of the Bible,* Supplementary Volume, ed. Keith Crim. Nashville: Abingdon Press, 1976, 763–71.

Toorn, K. van der. *Sin and Sanction in Israel and Mesopotamia: A Comparative Study.* Assen/Maastricht: Van Gorcum, 1985.

Turner, Victor. "Sacrifice as Quintessential Process: Prophylaxis or Abandonment?" *History of Religions* 16 (1977): 189–215.

Wenham, Gordon J. *The Book of Leviticus.* Grand Rapids: Eerdmans, 1979.

Zohar, Noam. "Repentance and Purification: The Significance and Semantics of *ḥṭ't* in the Pentateuch." *Journal of Biblical Literature* 107 (1988): 609–18.

CHAPTER ELEVEN

Chaney, Marvin L. "Debt Easement in Old Testament History and Tradition." In *The Bible and the Politics of Exegesis: Essays in Honor of Norman K. Gottwald,* ed. David Jobling, Peggy Day, and Gerald T. Sheppard. New York: Pilgrim Press, 1991.

Couroyer, B. "ʿEDUT: Stipulation de traité ou enseignement?" *Revue biblique* 95 (1988): 321–31.

Finkelstein, J.J. "Ammisaduqa's Edict and the Babylonian 'Law Codes.' " *Journal of Cuneiform Studies* 15 (1961): 91–104.

———. "Some New *misharum* Material and its Implications." In *Studies in Honor of Benno Landsberger.* Assyriological Studies, 16. Chicago: University of Chicago Press, 1965, 233–46.

Lewy, Julius. "The Biblical Institution of *deror* in the Light of Akkadian Documents." *Eretz-Israel* 5 (1958): 21*-31*.

North, R. *Sociology of the Biblical Jubilee.* Rome: Pontifical Biblical Institute Press, 1954.

Patrick, Dale. *Old Testament Law.* Atlanta: John Knox Press, 1985, 145–88, "The Holiness Code and Priestly Law."

van Selms, Adrianus. "Jubilee, Year of." In *Interpreter's Dictionary of the Bible,* Supplementary Volume, ed. Keith Crim. Nashville: Abingdon Press, 1976, 496–98.

von Rad, Gerhard. *Old Testament Theology.* Vol. 1. New York: Harper & Row, 1962, 232–79.

CHAPTER TWELVE

Countryman, L. William. *Dirt, Greed, and Sex: Sexual Ethics in the New Testament and Their Implications for Today.* Philadelphia: Fortress Press, 1988.

Daly, Robert J. *The Origins of the Christian Doctrine of Sacrifice*. Philadelphia: Fortress Press, 1978.

Eilberg-Schwartz, Howard. "Creation and Classification in Judaism: From Priestly to Rabbinic Conceptions." *History of Religions* 26 (1986/87): 357–81.

Fallon, Frank T. *The Enthronement of Sabaoth: Jewish Elements in Gnostic Creation Myths*. Leiden: E. J. Brill, 1978.

Pagels, Elaine. "Exegesis and Exposition of the Genesis Creation Accounts in Selected Texts from Nag Hammadi." In *Nag Hammadi, Gnosticism, and Early Christianity,* ed. Charles W. Hedrick and Robert Hodgson, Jr. Peabody: Hendrickson, 1986, 257–85.

Ringe, Sharon H. *Jesus, Liberation, and the Biblical Jubilee*. Philadelphia: Fortress, 1985.

Sanders, James A. "From Isaiah 61 to Luke 4." In *Christianity, Judaism, and Other Greco-Roman Cults: Studies for Morton Smith at Sixty.* Part I: New Testament, ed. Jacob Neusner. Leiden: Brill, 1975, 75–106.

EPILOGUE

Levenson, Jon D. *Creation and the Persistence of Evil: The Jewish Drama of Divine Omnipotence*. San Francisco: Harper & Row, 1988.

Niditch, Susan. *Creation to Cosmos: Studies in Biblical Patterns of Creation*. Chico: Scholars Press, 1985.

Westermann, Claus. *Creation*. Philadelphia: Fortress Press, 1974.

Author Index

Albright, W. F., 99
Andreasen, N. A., 81 n.5

Barnouin, M., 85 n.15
Bird, P., 72–73
Borowski, O., 93
Braudel, F., 58
Brichto, H. C., 110, 115, 151
Brueggemann, W., 55 n.4

Caplice, R., 12
Chaney, M., 124 n.5
Cohen, J., 55 n.4
Colson, F. H., 83
Coogan, M., 16–18, 98–99
Countryman, L. W., 144 n.3
Couroyer, B., 102 n.13
Cross, F. M., 40 n.3, 84, 97, 99, 100,
    102 n.14, 122 n.3
Cryer, F. H., 40 n.3, 45 n.13

Emerton, J., 40 n.3

Finkelstein, J. J., 126, 127–28
Fishbane, M., 26
Friedman, R. E., 40 n.3, 43, 44, 99–
    100
Frymer-Kensky, T., 13 n.13, 46

Gaster, T. H., 109 n.2, 112
Geller, M. J., 112
Gellner, E., 35–36

Goodman, M., 140
Gottwald, N., 139
Gruber, M. I., 71 n.8, 73 n.12

Hallo, W. H., 81 n.5, 83, 84 n.13
Haran, M., 40 n.3
Harris, M., 64 n.3
Heidel, A., 7, 8, 9, 10, 13
Hesse, B., 65 n.3
Hillers, D. R., 84, 101–2
Hopkins, D. C., 93
Hübner, U., 65 n.3
Hurowitz, V., 97

Jay, N., 109 n.2

Kearney, P., 85 n.15, 96–97
Kilmer, A., 12
Knauf, E. A., 39 n.1, 44 n.10
Koch, K., 40 n.3

Lemaire, A., 80–81, 84–85

McCarthy, D., 111
McEwan, G. J. P., 106–7
Milgrom, J., 112, 113

Oakman, D., 145

Paige, K. E. and J. M., 68–70
Pettinato, G., 13
Polley, M. E., 25 n.5

Tsevat, M., 83 n.11
Tsumura, D. T., 51 n.2

Wenham, G., 31 n.3, 71 n.8, 112, 114

Zevit, Z., 40 n.3, 46
Zohar, N., 112

Subject Index

Aaronids, 33, 36–38, 39, 43–44, 49.
  See also Zadokites
Abraham, 37, 41–42, 43, 60, 67–68
Amos, 25–26, 118
Atrahasis, 11

Baal, 16–18, 20, 98
Bezalel, 88, 89, 95–96, 98, 163. *See
  also* Craftsmen
Blood, 46, 54, 56, 58–59, 70–72, 106,
  108
Bow (rainbow), 59, 60

Circumcision, 37, 60, 67–70, 73–75,
  147–48
Clean and unclean, 45, 57, 59–66, 71–
  73, 152–53
Covenant, 43, 58–60, 67, 72–75, 77,
  86–88, 145, 148–49
Craftsmen, 8, 16–17, 20–21, 89–90,
  96, 98
Creation
  as establishment of temple/cult, 7–
    8, 10, 14, 17–18, 20, 22–24
  by division of waters, 7, 9, 14, 17,
    20, 21–24, 53
  by word of command, 14–15, 27–
    28, 51–52, 155
  of humanity, 7, 8, 9, 11–13, 27, 54–
    55
  of light and lights, 24–28, 50, 52–
    53, 82
Creation stories, 5

from Egypt, 13–16
from Mesopotamia, 6–13. *See also*
  Enuma elish
from Ugarit, 16–18, 98–99
Creationism, ix, 1, 3
Cult, 6, 13, 20, 26, 31, 49, 108, 113,
  118. *See also* Creation

D (Deuteronomistic history), 29–30,
  34–35, 37–38
David, house of, 29, 32–33, 34, 35,
  39 n.1, 99–101
Debt easement, 92, 124–29, 130–31.
  See also Jubilee

E strand, 29, 40, 41 n.1
El, 16, 82, 97–99, 101, 122
Elite ruling class, 5, 8, 9, 15, 30–32,
  49, 84–85, 123, 131–33
Enuma elish, 8, 50, 81
Ephesians, 143
Exodus, 19–20, 86–90
Ezekiel, 34, 39 n.1, 93, 101, 102, 120
Ezra, 37

Flood, 11–12, 45

Genesis 1, 1–4, 19, 28, 29, 38, 49, 66,
  146–48, 155
Gilgamesh, 11

Haggai, 96
Hebrews, letter to, 157–58

Herod the Great, 138–40
Hezekiah, 33

Isaiah, 21, 22, 36, 85, 102, 132–33

J strand, 29, 40, 41 n.4
JE, 40–47, 100
Jeremiah, 24–25, 34, 35, 85, 119–20,
    126–27
Jesus, 140, 144–46
Job, 22, 96
Joel, 119
John, Gospel of, 155–57
Josiah, 34, 36, 124
Jubilee, 92, 125, 128–31, 133, 154
Jurisdiction, 5, 26, 30–32, 141–42,
    162
Justice, 26, 60, 108, 112–13, 115, 117–
    24, 145, 154–56

Kavod, 102–4, 120

Land tenure, 5, 124, 128–29, 132, 153
Law, 32, 34, 37, 41, 60, 87–89, 90,
    93, 120–24, 153, 156
Levites, 32, 34, 36–38
Leviticus, 59–64, 90–93, 110–13,
    121–25
Luke-Acts, 143, 153–55

Maccabees, 135–39
Mark, Gospel of, 140, 144, 149–52
Matthew, Gospel of, 153
Meat eating, 31, 54, 58–66, 85, 106–
    7
Moses, 32–33, 34, 42, 43, 59, 60, 88

Nehemiah, 28, 38, 85

Noah, 11, 41–42, 43, 45, 56, 58–59,
    148–49

P strand, ix, 29, 36, 38, 39–47, 85–
    86, 162
Paul, 143–44, 146–49
Pentateuch, 29–30, 140
Persians, 35–38, 39, 49, 85, 117, 131–
    32
Pharisees, 137–39, 140, 144–46, 157
Priests, 5, 30–38, 61, 72–73, 117, 138,
    159. *See also* Aaronids, Levites,
    Zadokites
Psalms, 21, 23, 26–28, 121
Purification, 46, 111–12

Reproduction, 12, 54–55, 68–69, 74

Sabbath, 56, 60, 77–93, 96, 145, 152
Sacrifice, 20, 31, 60, 105–15
Sadducees, 137, 139–42
Sea, battle with, 9, 16, 19–20, 21–24,
    51, 53, 150
Seven (number), 41, 77–78, 79–84,
    91, 96

Tabernacle, 42, 60, 89–90, 95–104,
    108, 155
Temple, 5, 20–21, 22, 30–32, 36, 97,
    100–101, 120, 132–33, 138–45,
    149–52, 155–57
Tent, 20, 98, 99–102. *See also* Tab-
    ernacle
Torah, 37, 39, 135, 140, 142–43, 145,
    148, 157
Tribute (temple tax), 31, 113–15, 132

Zadokites, 32, 33–35, 38–39